THE
MAGA
DOCTRINE

THE
MAGA
DOCTRINE

The Only Ideas That
Will Win the Future

Charlie Kirk

BROADSIDE BOOKS
An Imprint of HarperCollinsPublishers

HarperCollins books may be purchased for educational, business, or sales promotional use. For information, please email the Special Markets Department at SPsales@harpercollins.com.

Broadside Books™ and the Broadside logo are trademarks of HarperCollins Publishers.

FIRST EDITION

Library of Congress Cataloging-in-Publication Data has been applied for.

ISBN 978-0-06-297468-6

20 21 22 23 24   LSC   10 9 8 7 6 5 4 3 2 1

To President Donald J. Trump.

You came, you saw, you fixed. Thank you for the sacrifices you've made and continue to make. You're putting our nation on the right track by ending wars, making government smaller, and enabling Americans to succeed.

Contents

Preface: What Is the MAGA Doctrine?

Americans don't like to be told what to do. By anybody.

They don't want their options limited by social justice warriors, EPA busybodies, or UN blowhards. They didn't like Jimmy Carter telling them to put on a sweater and turn down the thermostat, and they didn't like Michelle Obama lecturing them on what to eat. The entire elite political class is obsessed with lecturing their constituents. In fact, Donald Trump may be the first president in any of our lifetimes who doesn't periodically take to the bully pulpit to tell us how to live our lives.

At every turn, Americans are told they are breaking the rules, written and unwritten, both legal and moral. This is a strange fate for a people whose nation was built upon individual liberty and a historic break with old-world tyranny.

Liberty is the shield with which we have protected individuals, families, churches, and communities—including groups that can't easily fight back by themselves.

Accompanying liberty is a healthy dose of skepticism about authority figures and experts who think they know best. That skepticism sometimes means listening to one wise farmer instead of a UN or EPA agriculture committee when regulations are suggested. It may mean listening to one online voice instead of the Silicon Valley cartel united against him—or one conservative professor censured by a left-wing Ivy League university. (Even the left understands this, even if they swear they don't. They recently elected a bartender to Congress, after all, and claimed that was what made her worth listening to.)

A people this rebellious do not take kindly either to a government that intrudes into every area of our lives (in the name of everything from defense to ending poverty, while achieving neither)—nor do we take kindly to a media elite that tells us we can't vote for an outsider presidential candidate. They can bury us in fake news aimed at training us to hate that outsider candidate, but Americans still don't like to be told what to do.

In fact, that outsider candidate may start to sound more like a fellow rebel to them than like a threat.

The MAGA Doctrine is a book about what happens when the two political parties stop listening to the people and the people win anyway. We live in a democratic republic, but this is still a near miracle. We will examine how the most controversial president of modern times managed to transform American politics in just a few years and how politicians and pundits raced to keep up.

Throughout the stories of policy wins and political battles, we will explore two key ideas. The first is the false
claim that Trump's political base is not forward-thinking.
The slogan Make America Great Again may use the past
as the benchmark for greatness, but we are not advocating
a return to mid-century America. Turn on the television
or read newspaper columns calling modern conservatives
backward-looking, and you can see why they consistently
get President Trump wrong. They misread what is happening. They offer false predictions on what will happen next.

If you think we are not calling for a brighter future as a
strong, dynamic country of free and equal Americans, you
will never understand the revolution happening before your
eyes.

Heading into the 2016 election, both parties assumed the
presidency would be decided on the same old issues, presented in the same boring way. They prepared accordingly.
The Republican base found a better choice, and caught a
dying Democrat Party off guard.

Why has there been so much misunderstanding around
the president's popularity and plans? In the pages that follow, I'm going to argue that even members of his own party
continue to misunderstand the permanence of the change
among the base.

That brings us to the second, deeper idea here. Critics of
the president can't see that the giant, lumbering institutions
they run—from the Deep State to the *New York Times*—
are the ones not well prepared for the future. The reasons
they feel so smug about running the country for decades to
come are, in fact, the reasons they will soon lose control of
everything.

They find Trump's constant battles against the urban elite puzzling. A television celebrity attacking the media? A billionaire attacking billionaires? A Manhattanite in a suit winning over stadiums full of farmers? What they don't understand is that the masses have been looking for someone to stand up to the powerful, and who else could get away with it? Trump may be the freest man in the world.

What is the MAGA Doctrine? Bigger is not always better. The role of government should be so small that it is barely noticeable. Yet, over the past several decades it has ballooned into an enormous enterprise thanks to both political parties. Too many institutions created to counter the power of government, from the media to Wall Street, have practically joined forces with it. Fake news is out of control and defense contractors have taken unprecedented advantage of the American taxpayer.

Protecting individual liberty from the tyrannical forces of government is the idea our nation was built upon. It is the only way to protect the individual's rights, the family, local churches and schools, and other groups who can't fight back themselves.

Be skeptical of everything, especially your government. Ask questions, fight for your rights, and never surrender.

President Trump has been under attack from the moment he declared he was running. Neither electoral challenges nor impeachment threats can erase the Trump legacy. He has brought about a reawakening. I have actually been a supporter of Donald Trump since well before his 2016 presidential campaign. Way back in 2011, I tweeted to him, "Run Trump Run! Your country needs you!" I guess you could say I was MAGA before it was cool. I was thrilled eight years later when, as president, Donald Trump said, "I want to thank Charlie. He's an incredible guy. His spirit, his love of this country. He's done an amazing job."

From the first time I briefly met Donald Trump Jr., son of the future president, at the 2016 Republican National Convention to my hosting events through the organization I founded, Turning Point USA (themselves drawing tens of thousands of student activist participants), the past few years have been an amazing journey.

Now, I should reveal the philosophy motivating it all—and motivating the president.

Turning Point USA started before the Trump 2016 presidential campaign but exploded in size around that time, as the student activists who make up the group's ranks began to hope that they might soon have a president who heard their voices. The group doesn't exist just to cheer on one politician—our well-attended annual events such as the Teen Student Action Summit, Young Black Leadership Summit, and Young Jewish Leadership Summit attest to that. We are strictly an educational organization dedicated to preaching the values of free markets, the Constitution, and American exceptionalism.

But Turning Point USA participants, including former Turning Point USA staff member and BLEXIT founder Candace Owens, have a shared philosophical impulse, and a basic political desire, that is roughly summed up in President Trump's slogan, seen on the ubiquitous red hats of his supporters: Make America Great Again, abbreviated MAGA. As I will explain, MAGA is more than just a slogan. There is a set of principles, however roughly hewn, behind the president's vision of national renewal—one that is both familiar and eternally in need of clear, firm restatement. The MAGA

Doctrine didn't spring into existence in 2016—because it is the core philosophy by which our whole society has come to be over several centuries.

I've seen President Trump speak in front of high school students, my fellow young conservative activists eager to hear him—and afterward, I often hear students ask me, is there a key book or manifesto I can study to really understand the philosophy behind this burgeoning movement? Behind this rising new sensibility that is partly conservative, partly libertarian, partly populist, partly nationalist, and yet not just an old-fashioned, textbook case of any of these strains of thought? Now there is. I would not presume to speak for the president, but I will try as best I can to explain the old ideas underlying the fresh thinking he brings to a country that desperately needs it.

One important reason to offer a defense of the MAGA Doctrine as Donald Trump faces reelection is that if those of us who support him do not make our case, our political opponents will not hesitate to "explain" the MAGA Doctrine for us. We know what their description of our philosophy will be: Trump supporters are racist. Trump himself is a fascist. Trump's policies fly in the face of common sense and shred the Constitution.

They will claim our thinking is un-American even as they trash the American traditions of liberty and limited government they claim to be defending. These elites deride Trump supporters even as their own philosophy threatens to demolish the very things that made America great.

What philosophy is considered hip among many people from my millennial generation? Socialism! One of the most disastrous ideologies ever devised. To that rival faction in particular, I offer these stats (some of the many such facts I like to share on my Twitter feed and podcast):

Two hundred years ago,

- 84% of the world lived in extreme poverty. Today, 90% don't.
- 83% didn't have a basic education. Today, 86% do.
- 1% lived in a democracy. Today just 44% don't.
- The child mortality rate was 43%. Today, it's 4%.

All thanks to the free market socialists want to destroy. If anything, economic growth rates and progress have slowed in the past few decades as the welfare state, to which the socialists give all the credit for such advances, grew. The new socialists and Democrats steadfastly ignore these facts. And it is this delusion that makes the MAGA Doctrine more important than ever.

The MAGA Doctrine is, in part, a path back to the brave, pioneering spirit that made not just survival but explosive growth and visionary changes possible in America. Join me now in tracing that past and pointing the way, with Trump's help, to an even brighter future.

THE
MAGA
DOCTRINE

CHAPTER 1

The Great Disruptor

Two days after Trump won the 2016 election, I found myself up in famed Trump Tower in New York City, invited by Tommy Hicks of the America First PAC, who is now co-chair of the Republican National Committee. I was in the building in part to see if Donald Trump Jr. had been serious when he said during the campaign that he wanted to help draw attention to my organization, Turning Point USA. Plenty of politicians and their relatives are eager to be your friend during a hard-fought campaign but ditch you—and everything for which you stood—once they've secured their victory.

In fact, Donald Jr. famously said during the campaign, when I offered to help spread the word about his father, that the last thing the campaign needed was another person too young and inexperienced to know much about campaigning. Would he be dismissive now, despite promising to help?

But Donald Jr. was as good as his word and plugged my efforts by thanking me for our role in his father's victory. That connection helped spur the amazing growth of Turning Point USA over the past three years. The group had existed for a few years before that, but it was increasingly clear it would be a vehicle for the shifting mood in the country, and in particular the shifting hopes of young people who for so long had been taught the left owns the future and is the only natural vehicle for the rising generations' political aspirations.

Don Jr. understood that the next generation matters. All too often our youth are exposed to liberal ideas at school, at college, on television, and online without any counterbalance. Groups such as Turning Point USA provide an alternative. Accompanying Don when he appeared at events with a big Turning Point USA presence would often be his smart and beautiful girlfriend, Kimberly Guilfoyle, who always helped get the crowd fired up. A former prosecutor and a natural speaker, Guilfoyle spent a decade hosting the highest-rated shows on Fox News before joining the Trump campaign to assist with the 2020 reelection.

With the moral support of a few such allies, in the past few years Turning Point USA has gone from a budget of about $2 million per year to $20 million per year, enabling us to have an ongoing presence on some 1,600 campuses, about 70% of them colleges and 30% high schools. Our annual December conference draws about 3,500 students. A big part of that growth has been the general Trump political momentum, but the kind words and helpful advice of Don Jr. and Ivanka in particular have made a palpable difference.

I would like to think maybe Donald Jr. sees in me and in Turning Point USA something just a little like his dad: a force for disruption, one the old guard resents sometimes because it shows up the hollowness of that old guard's prior efforts. Like President Trump, we have tried to combat decades of political "conventional wisdom" with common sense.

I can understand political intellectuals being reluctant to admit that Donald Trump has changed the course of American politics. Big changes in politics are "supposed" to come from longtime party leaders, philosophers, professors, experts, think tanks, elite intellectual cliques. How could one man, even riding an immense (and indeed global) wave of populist sentiment, possibly shatter our longstanding political models and arguably rewrite the political spectrum?

One key to Trump's success is that he sensed how terribly out of touch with its constituents the political establishment had become. It's his job to notice market opportunities, and the two major political parties, foolishly, had created a big one. Think of the way Fox News viewers embraced Trump quicker than the pundits and producers of Fox did. Think of how pained the pundit class was at his verbal sparring with Fox host Megyn Kelly and yet how readily her viewers sided with him. Even at that solidly conservative network, in other words, there was a gap between what the public was thinking and what the experts were saying in their name. The conservative experts—the talking heads—were espousing an old party line that, though it has a venerable history, may not resonate so much anymore.

The gridlock that the two major parties had fallen into, and the tired repetition in their messages, may have been an inevitable long-term side effect of the majority-rule structure of our democracy. The two parties were not written into the Constitution, and it was several decades before their organization and names were even formal, as opposed to names for loose and shifting coalitions of legislators. But if an absolute majority of electoral college votes is required to win the presidency and winner-take-all has been the norm in both national and state elections, one governing coalition—regardless of its stated ideology—has an incentive to try to win just over 50% of public support, while the other governing coalition has an incentive to do the same. Eventual gridlock may be the inevitable destiny of any majority-rules democratic system.

And then the two dominant coalitions, now formalized as two semi-permanent parties—the Democrats and the Republicans in our case—start getting used to each other. Far too used to each other. They squabble. The party with the upper hand and the party with the lower hand in current national affairs shift slightly from time to time, but a 50/50 stalemate starts to seem just, well, natural. Probably permanent.

Once those two parties get comfortable, resigned to the fact that neither is ever going to completely destroy the other, they can get down to furthering shared interests—"horse trading for votes," as the saying goes. You give my district something big at the taxpayers' expense in the next appropriations bill, which my district will thank me for, and I'll give your district something expensive that they'll thank you for.

A two-party cartel, entrenched and self-serving, soon looks like the most natural manifestation of democracy imaginable.

The heads of those two parties argue when they must, each party hoping to differentiate itself from the other just enough to eke out a victory in the next election—but neither wants to argue for, or if elected institute, change so fundamental that it would destroy all the stuff that the leaders of the two parties have in common with each other and not with you, the general public: unearned use of $4 trillion a year, the power to regulate, and the endless attention of fawning lobbyists and Washington powerbrokers.

Both parties, to varying degrees, have favored a large welfare/regulatory state and constant military interventions overseas. We see each of the two parties talking to itself, regurgitating the same rhetoric decade after decade, and changing essentially nothing about governance itself aside from letting spending levels constantly inch slightly upward, debt constantly deepen, and the military, frustratingly, bloat and age at the same time.

There is an unholy alliance between the left and the right. The left wants welfare spending and the right wants more military spending. The result is both sides come together in a bipartisan fashion and increase spending on both. As the losing 2016 presidential candidate might say, "What difference does it make?"

Is it any shock, really, that in 2016 George H. W. Bush proudly announced that he voted for Hillary Clinton instead of Trump? Even though Bush's own son, hapless Jeb, had wanted to defeat Clinton, in the end the Bushes and Clintons were like two branches of one big happy family, merely rotating who got a turn in the Oval Office this time out. How collegial.

Trump was the first real disruption to that decrepitude in a long, long time.

■ ■ ■

It helped maintain the two-party cartel if the two major parties, Democrats and Republicans, pretended, at least around
election time, to be complete, diametrical opposites, even
though the leadership of both parties would be sharing mar-
tinis and crafting pork-filled legislation together with knowing winks as soon as the every-two-years or every-four-years
mock-battle was over.

But the two parties were never quite literally *opposites* in
their philosophies.

The old Democrat formula, ideally stated, was something
like: a big welfare and regulatory state combined with an
American military subordinated to big international alliances
and treaty organizations.

The old Republican formula, ideally stated, was something like: free trade, big business, opposition to welfare,
legislation defending traditional morality (such as pushing
for pro-life measures when possible), plus never-ending military engagements overseas, with every dictator around the
world due to become our fighting foe eventually.

This two-party faceoff has changed a little on the left in
recent years—and the situation has changed drastically on
the right thanks to President Trump.

The Democratic formula arguably once included respect for
civil liberties and a welfare state that, however dysfunctional,
was rooted in the moderate American understanding that it's
great to ensure everyone's basic needs are met and that each
person can go out and make his or her own way in the world.
The new Democratic formula, exaggerating those impulses,
appears to be moral relativism and flat-out socialism. Oh, they
told us for decades that they weren't socialists, just "liberals" (a

once-honorable term that meant a believer in free markets and limited government back in the nineteenth century), but half of Democratic primary voters picking avowed socialist Bernie Sanders in the party's 2016 primaries seems to put the lie to that distinction, as do the enthusiastic cries that socialist loud-mouths such as Representative Alexandria Ocasio-Cortez are the "future of the party."

The Democrats, in short, appear to be getting worse—and as long as they could point to the rich, crony-capitalist Republicans with their eagerly doled-out corporate subsidies as the only alternative, the Democrats could still be pretty well assured they had nothing big, at least nothing fatal in the long run, to fear in the electoral arena. They could still present themselves as the great defenders of the working class, the only party really checking in on the common folk as the economy had its ups and downs. The blue-collar, average-American choice.

And a rising tide of immigration could only help, the demographics favoring the Democrats, and almost no one on the Republican side was really willing to risk a potentially ugly fight on that topic. Too divisive, too offensive. The establishment Republicans, with no real, heartfelt governing philosophy anyway, might as well sit back and enjoy the long, slow ride to irrelevance and try not to sound too different from the Democrats during the process.

Still, even among political philosophers, the assumption remained that as one moved leftward along a linear political axis, one grew more internationalist, more welfare-statist, and more comfortable with personal liberties such as free speech. As one moved rightward, one became more theocratic, more militaristic, more pro-establishment, more morally uptight, and more skeptical about free speech.

Then came Trump.

After decades of assuming that the two-party stasis meant the leaders of each party could keep dictating the same positions to the rank and file, Republican Party leaders were startled in 2016 to discover that their constituents wanted something else. The new de facto party platform would be trade with a dash of strategic protectionism, free speech, and skepticism about the use of military power overseas—combined with a desire to avoid socialism at home, avoid the erosion of our core culture, and avoid subsidizing other countries when our own has unmet needs.

Trump has swept aside an astonishing number of conservative taboos, once-dominant institutions, and once-unbreakable rules through the sheer force of his personality—and the emphatic truths of the MAGA Doctrine.

As Trump economic advisor Stephen Moore put it in a blunt speech to Republican House members, the Republican Party is in some sense no longer a conservative party, no longer the party of Reagan, but instead a Trump-remade populist party.

Trump's list of priorities—and in many ways they are uniquely his (aside from some populists whose ideas slightly resemble his in some areas and not at all in others, such as Pat Buchanan)—redefines what "conservatism" or "the right" is, offering a new Republican formula, a marked improvement over the old Republican formula, in contrast to the trajectory of decline in the Democratic Party.

If old Democrat was something like civil liberties/ welfare/internationalism and new Democrat is something like censorship/socialism/internationalism, while old Republican was something like theocratic/corporate/ warlike, then the new Republican formula is roughly free speech/entrepreneurial/pro-peace.

Not all change is good, but this is. Even founding conservative thinker Edmund Burke recognized that some changes can serve to conserve what is best about a society and its regime. Burke endorsed the American Revolution, in fact, whereas one might have expected a British conservative to say the king can never err. True conservatives recognize when things have gotten so bad that change is necessary. Those who don't care about rescuing a society may just stay along for the ride as the whole thing goes over a cliff.

The height of Republican decadence, in a way, was the neoconservative movement. It had respectable roots, with great thinkers such as Irving Kristol defending basic conservative moral principles at a time of moral relativism and political chaos in the 1960s, and the neoconservatives were stalwart defenders of Reagan and critics of communism. However, people in power will start getting cocky eventually, and by the time of George W. Bush's presidency, neoconservatives such as William Kristol were talking not just about defending America (a noble goal, obviously) but about asserting "American Empire" all over the globe. They were also quite open about not wanting to waste too much time on free markets or the rhetoric of individualism—the libertarian part of the conservative movement.

The neoconservatives, in publications such as the now-defunct magazine the *Weekly Standard*, defended grotesque ideas such as "big-government conservatism," preferring founding Progressive Teddy Roosevelt to free-marketeers such as Steve Forbes, all the while claiming that they were promoting "National Greatness." America was indeed in need of a renewal of its greatness, but fighting long, bloody, expensive wars in Afghanistan and Iraq was not the way to Make America Great Again. Maybe if we had more quickly and decisively won those wars, the story would be different. But as candidate Trump so simply and insightfully put it, "We don't win anymore."

A house-cleaning was necessary, and it is stunning how many old, fossilized things Trump swept aside on his path to electoral victory and national renewal, how many things he continues to sweep aside, things we thought surely no Republican could win without. He dismissed the *Weekly Standard*, he questioned the conservative bona fides of some *National Review* writers, he was skeptical of John McCain's war record, he sometimes argued with Fox News (despite recurring leftist claims that that's where he gets all his ideas).

Who could have imagined back when I was born, in the 1990s, that the Republican Party might become the vehicle for opposing endless warfare? This is change. This is disruption, right down to the very foundations of modern political ideology.

Furthermore, Trump is obviously no prude (though his optimistic, Norman Vincent Peale–influenced religion-plus-business streak stayed with him during his election campaign, even as secular critics hypocritically questioned his Christian credentials). Trump has probably become the greatest living exemplar of free speech in the twenty-first century. As he put it, we can't improve if political correctness prevents us from even talking honestly about what our problems are.

It's not that those of us on Team Trump long to be rude. It's not that we look down on any subsets of American society. All individuals are created equal—but not all cultures and ideas are equal, and we need to be able to compare and contrast intelligently. Yet the left, with its warped and doctrinaire version of equality, really wants to replace the Founding ideas of striving, competition, and individual excellence with mediocrity, enforced mediocrity if necessary—and that's not how America became great. It's not how America is being made great again.

The tragedy of the left is that while they may envision, or claim to envision, an America of happy equals, they also want endless conflict—anger instead of gratitude. They want people to be offended instead of being civil. What better way than to convince the populace that every advantage another citizen has over you, earned or unearned, real or imagined, is offensive and must be taken away? Who but the biggest of big governments will ever have the power to impose the entire anti-meritocratic leftist vision on society? I think on some level, they know their vision is unworkable, and they like the fact that it will leave the public frustrated and angry, ready to be stirred up and led against the next common enemy, just as they have tried to rally Americans against Trump, in whom they thought they had the perfect, easily defeated villain.

Trump was saying the forbidden things that the two-party cartel had for so long rendered, by mutual agreement, unspeakable. And it turned out these weren't things that Americans were horrified to hear. Once they got over the shock—once they recovered from some sharp insults and salty language—they realized Trump was articulating the things most of us take for granted and had long suppressed: competence matters, intelligence matters, American independence matters, defying the pretended authorities of media or state matters.

The MAGA Doctrine is no mere return to nineteenth-century racism or narrow-mindedness, as should by now be obvious. It is something new, but if it must be likened to a prior era, or at least one aspect of a prior era, think of the great social mobility of the 1980s, when prosperity and newfound financial independence helped make full citizens at last of women and ethnic minorities so often left out before—even as the end of European Communism helped spread notions of entrepreneurship and individual freedom to places long deprived of them.

The Trump plan is not to undo any of those gains but to build upon them. It is not the imposition of a strongman but, quite the contrary, the restoration of citizen government after too many decades of that two-party cartel thinking it barely needed to answer to the people.

The Democrats cannot mouth the same old slogans and take it for granted that everyone will believe they are the only spokesmen for the poor and the workers. They know Trump speaks to those Americans as well.

The Republicans cannot take it for granted that by the occasional salute to the soldiers or bowing of the head in prayer they will pass for true patriots and saintly neighbors. They know Trump has called their bluffs and shown Americans want greatness without needless war, belief without restricting speech.

This is a liberation of America long overdue—and it may be the last chance to institute it, with the socialists and the stale corporatists still looming to the left and right. I hope we will not reverse course in the 2020 election. America really is, if I may borrow a phrase, at a turning point.

That phrase suggests that the group I run isn't just about opinions but about action. Disrupting the old coalitions is much more painful than just repeating old arguments or phrasing them in a new way. I'm an activist, not just a pundit—in much the same way that President Trump is someone who wants to get things done, not just stake out his ideological territory. You, too, can be an activist, and this book may help inspire you in that regard, but you will meet, to coin a phrase, resistance—and not always where you expect it.

I do not go out of my way to make enemies—and I have great respect for the long line of conservative thinkers who have made my tentative contribution to politics possible—but sometimes the most vicious opposition to me, to Turning Point USA, and to Trump himself has come from the right, not the left. The left, after all, has an exciting new enemy to fight in the Trump era. Many on the pre-Trump right need to rethink their lives and ask if they still have a purpose. Most do, but some have to confess they were going about things entirely the wrong way, maybe even enjoying the endless stalemate between right and left, not really holding out any realistic hope of winning or causing change.

Some folks at the older, established "conservative" publications have even made Turning Point USA sound like a nuisance, an upstart. They accuse us of watering down timeless principles to create mere clickbait. They say we aren't bringing in intellectually qualified recruits. Every movement bigger than your living room will have a few embarrassing members, and every media and political organization fights to get attention in the modern media environment, but I think Turning Point USA's real "crime" is that we expose how ineffectual the old ways had become and show that new audiences and bigger political victories are possible if people get a little more imaginative and provocative.

Those complaints about Turning Point USA have some parallels, obviously, in the complaints from most of the conservative establishment when the Trump campaign first started picking up steam, defying the predictions of all the revered experts. Trump won't last, he isn't serious, he's just stirring up the yahoo vote, and so on.

But as union leader Nicholas Klein said in 1918 (if I may borrow a line from the left), "First they ignore you. Then they ridicule you. And then they attack you and want to burn you. And then they build monuments to you." I try to resist the urge to tell the older conservative groups, "I told you so." We just keep moving ahead instead of wasting too much time fighting old rivals we've already eclipsed.

If the old conservative approaches were flawless, the whole world wouldn't have been convinced in 2016 that Hillary Clinton's presidency was an inevitability, and the pundits wouldn't have thought that Jeb Bush was the farthest the right could safely stray from liberal orthodoxy in its thinking. Trump saw that these assumptions were a failure of imagination—and he knew the Republicans were making an immense, long-term tactical mistake because he talked to normal Americans outside the media/politics bubble. He heard and shared the average American's worries about mass immigration, the shrinking middle class, thousands of friends and neighbors being wounded in wars that no one talked about winning anymore, and the ever-increasing restrictions on what we can say and think without sparking outrage.

Why would a party establishment ignore those longings—and those votes—unless it were severely out of touch or just didn't share the common person's values anymore? The elites of both parties had developed beliefs and goals of their own, often antithetical to the public's.

But now let's take a look at some of the deeper, older false assumptions the Trump movement has demolished.

CHAPTER 2

The Outsider from the Inside

Imagine for a minute if Donald Trump had not won the 2016 presidential election.

Imagine instead if Hillary Clinton had won—the electoral college tally, the whole nine yards.

Next, just for the sake of argument, imagine if, during the first two years of her administration, she achieved stunning successes:

- The Dow rises 7,000 points after being nearly flat around 18,000 the two prior years.
- Consumer confidence surges to an eighteen-year high.
- Black unemployment hits 5.9%, the lowest level ever recorded.

- Hispanic and Asian-American unemployment also hit record lows of 4.5% and 2%, respectively.
- Female unemployment is at the lowest rate since 1953 (3.6%).
- Unemployment among the young is at its lowest in five decades (9.2%), among veterans the lowest in two (3%).
- Economic growth for the year nears 3% in 2018, for the first time since the 2008 financial crisis.
- There is a freeze on new regulations, to the relief of American businesses. For every new regulation, about twenty-two are repealed.
- Jobless claims are at their lowest level in five decades.
- Job openings outnumber people looking for jobs for the first time on record.
- The positive job-growth streak is the longest on record.
- Job satisfaction is at its highest level in a decade and a half, and 85% of blue-collar workers think the country is "headed in the right direction."
- Some $5.5 trillion in tax cuts are instituted, with most families seeing savings as a result.
- The corporate tax rate is lowered as well, since it had been the highest in the developed world and was discouraging investment.
- The president cleared bureaucratic obstacles to constructing the Keystone XL pipeline and withdrew from the onerous Paris Climate Agreement.
- The president helped make the United States the world's biggest crude oil exporter for the first time.
- ISIS's Iraq arm is effectively finished off.

- The United States stops funding Syrian militias with terror ties, quieting that country's civil war. Military conflicts in other parts of the world are largely avoided.
- NATO partner nations are successfully pressured into paying their fair share for the alliance, reducing the US burden.
- Sentencing reductions for nonviolent drug offenders are achieved, a big, libertarian step forward for criminal justice reform.
- Medical regulations are loosened to allow terminally ill patients to try experimental procedures if they so choose, approvals for affordable generic drugs are accelerated, and employers are permitted to create more flexible and varied health plans. Veterans' medical conditions are processed faster than ever before.
- The president entered the Oval Office already a supporter of gay marriage, the first US president of whom that is true.
- Two solidly conservative new Supreme Court justices are confirmed.
- Over five million new jobs are created, a half million in manufacturing and over a hundred thousand in oil and natural gas transportation.
- 95% of manufacturers say they are optimistic the country is headed in the right direction.

If our hypothetical President Hillary Rodham Clinton achieved all this, how might the press react? Even if the press disagreed with some of her policies and rhetoric, isn't it likely they would talk about her as competent, respectable, perhaps even an inspiration? How many schools and airports named after her would we have already? They might even call her track record "great," or at least acknowledge that she gets things done and knows how to deal with Capitol Hill. She would be praised as well by most academics and surely by advocates for the advancement of women.

Obviously and thankfully, Hillary Clinton never became president, but all of the achievements described above are real—and are the handiwork of the person who became president on January 20, 2017: Donald J. Trump. (Many of these items come from the *Washington Examiner*'s tally of Trump successes.)

Most of Washington can't comprehend how this could have happened. They're as perplexed by his achievements as they are by his giant crowds. They think they know what competence looks like: a four-hundred-dollar haircut and consultants telling you how not to make news. Never be funny. Take yourself too seriously for that. Meet as often as possible with other leaders who also have spent their careers trying not to generate headlines.

Where average Americans see in Trump an effort to restore greatness through opportunity and prosperity, the elite see someone alarming. If you can succeed in politics without the help of hundreds of lawyers, lobbyists, and reporters propping you up, an awful lot of members of the elite could be on the verge of losing their jobs.

However, the caricature of Trump as operating without a philosophical foundation is also wrong. Trump usually operates on what might be called instincts rather than detailed manifestos like those favored by some of his critics. But Trump's instincts did not arise in a vacuum. Like all Americans, he inherited a tradition that conveys the norms that have enabled us to flourish.

A lifetime as an entrepreneur taught him more about economics—and about the threat posed by an intrusive regulatory state—than is known by a fashionable socialist such as Representative Alexandria Ocasio-Cortez, despite the pride she takes in her economics degree.

He has lived in New York City at times of comfort and times of rampant crime, and he understands the importance of preventing violence, whether from Latin American drug cartels or radical Muslim terrorists. Most Americans understand that it is those profoundly decent impulses, not xenophobia, that inspire his sometimes harsh-sounding rhetoric about the need to protect our borders and crack down on real threats.

He understands the failings of the media because he was a media star. He understands the evil nature of some CEOs because he went to Wharton and has rubbed elbows with those people ever since. The scariest thing about him to the elite is that he has been inside with them, and he's exposing their secrets to the outside.

If he often sounds dismissive or impatient, it is not because he can brook no opposition but because, just like many of us, he is tired of seeing American ideals torn down. Unlike so many of his foes on the left, he's very grateful to this country for making possible all of his success. He's not a barbarian at the gates, to be fended off by the *New York Times* or the

Ivy League. Trump is a man already comfortably at home in America, at home with its people and its institutions. And the people sense that. They know he is one of them, not just another Washingtonian like all the ones he defeated and de-fied to become president.

If the establishment senses in our times something akin to ancient Rome, I suggest they look to a figure very different from Nero for Trump comparisons. They should look a cen-tury earlier, to the influential orator Cicero.

In a fashion eerily similar to the war against Trump waged by the American so-called Deep State (the govern-ment's permanent bureaucracy and more shadowy agencies, who sometimes act in defiance of the popular will), Cicero was declared an "enemy of the state" by Rome in the first century BC, not because he was a law-breaking hooligan but, on the contrary, because he warned that Rome was losing its way, ceasing to be great because it was straying from its long-held republican principles (republican with a small r, meaning characterized by sober deliberation, civic participation, virtue, and self-rule by the people).

Cicero came from a wealthy family, and through his oratory became what we might now dub a major media star in ancient Rome. He could have enjoyed a life of lux-ury and avoided conflict but regarded his foray into poli-tics, necessitated by his sense of civic duty, as his greatest achievement.

He spent much of that political career combating conspir-acies to overthrow the republic, in a fashion that might well be dismissed as paranoid by the complacent elitists of our own day. His fears were proven tragically correct, though, as Julius Caesar (sometimes talked about now as if he were the very pinnacle of Roman achievement but in truth a dictator who was the death knell of the Republic) pushed Rome in the direction of empire. Cicero himself ended up executed by government soldiers, his head and hands later displayed on Rome's central public speaking platform, a final taunt to Mark Antony—one of Caesar's allies, and after Caesar's assassination, part of Rome's ruling triumvirate.

When Trump-hating media star and CNN hostess/comedienne/filth-purveyor Kathy Griffin held up a fake bloodied Donald Trump head in a photo (subsequently being let go by CNN because of it), she may have been closer to the Rome-like truth than she realized—not because Trump is a dictator deserving death but because he, like Cicero, is targeted by powerful forces who mistake themselves for the Republic's protectors but are in fact in the process of destroying it.

Trump's battle, then, is not just a squabble with a few well-meaning, present-day liberal critics. He represents a centuries-long struggle within Western civilization between the hope of freedom and self-rule by the common people and the continual assertion of aristocratic privilege by those who think they know better and thus should have power. As long as Trump opposes those deeply entrenched forces, who not so secretly view America's Founding Fathers with almost as much suspicion and contempt as they view Trump, it will not matter how impressive his practical achievements in the economic or foreign policy realms are: They will still be denigrated and cast in a bad light because he is a threat to their own rule.

I have spent time with the Trump family, and I know President Trump is not a creature of whim or mere temper tantrums. He is guided by a faith that most Americans seemed to share until very recently. Our forefathers founded this country on sound principles, including standing up for the freedom of the individual. These principles with ancient roots have made something wonderful and new possible upon the face of the Earth, a freedom and prosperity never before known.

The smallest units of society—the individual, the family, the small business, the little towns, the local church and PTA—need to be protected with everything we've got.

When the noise of the current generation of pundits and analysts has long since faded away and historians assess the Trump presidency, I think they will see the broad strokes that his critics wish to deny. They will see the love of country, the defense of freedom, and the irreverence toward the false pieties of our day (and the elites who peddle them). They will also see a record of promises kept, after decades of Americans passively and glumly accepting that politics is all lies and false hopes.

Some of those future historians will be conservatives like the young people from Turning Point USA, which went in a few short years from being just an idea with barely any funding—a notion to connect rising high school and teen conservative activists into a supportive national network—to one of the most influential youth organizations in the world, hosting a speech by President Trump himself at our July 2019 conference. Those kids aren't fooled by the establishment narrative, and they're creating a better one.

The list of Trump achievements I noted is just the beginning of the greatness ahead. The MAGA Doctrine will continue to guide him through his second term, and will likely affect every president following him.

His critics have nothing to offer as inspiring and optimistic, as freedom-fostering and deeply humane. They will shift with the prevailing political winds, praising peace one day and unnecessary wars the next, choice one day and the heavy hand of regulation the next. Trump will stay true to his core principles.

We were constantly told in the three decades after the Cold War that the culture of Washington, D.C., couldn't be changed: The welfare state is permanent. Regulations must never be rolled back. Defense contractors keep getting their money no matter how many wars are declared over or almost over.

If only some outsider would shake things up, they'd say. Maybe a Ross Perot. Maybe an intellectual affiliated with neither major party. Maybe a mainstream politician rebranding himself as a "maverick." Maybe Barack Obama, with what he claimed would be an administration without ties to lobbyists.

As *Politico* put it, describing their own 2014 review of Trump's predecessor, "The Obama administration has hired more than 70 previously registered lobbyists . . . and watched many officials circle through that revolving door, as Obama's lobbying policy was weakened by major loopholes and a loss of focus over time. What's more, the current laws around lobbying, which the administration measures were built on, simply ignore many instances observers would regard as lobbying—and the White House never pressed for changes to those laws."

Now look at the panic once an outsider—who did not regard the culture of Washington with cautious respect—came along. You'd think Trump was a horde of invading Vandals from the way the media, politicians, and D.C. interest groups reacted to his election.

Was it because they opposed his ideas? Or was it because they knew he was irreverent enough and courageous enough to try changing Washington's ways—the codes of conduct, such as doing special favors for donors, that everyone lamented but no one really wanted to see changed because they were all benefiting from? Was Washington fearful Trump would make things worse or that he'd expose their past inaction and lamentations as phony, a little like Hollywood occasionally shedding crocodile tears over the world being too looks-obsessed and superficial, without for a moment wanting to operate in any other kind of world?

You won't know if you can fix Washington politics if you never really try. How many individuals have run and gotten elected to Congress, only to turn into the swamp creatures they led us to believe they would oppose? Champions of "smaller government" have grown government at an unprecedented rate. Few things are as permanent as a temporary government program. Individuals who campaigned on term limits have found themselves in the halls of Congress for decades on end, with no end in sight.

The Latin saying *Qui audet adipiscitur*—"Who dares, wins"—is evocative of Trump's ethos. The use of Latin is apt here, since historian Victor Davis Hanson argues that Trump's desire to Make America Great Again parallels the desire of several great leaders throughout history, including classical antiquity, to restore their own nations in periods of turbulence and corruption.

In a December 2018 interview with Hoover Institution's *The Classicist* podcast, Hanson likens the challenges that Trump faces to the ones that beset Emperor Justinian of the Byzantine Empire, the surviving eastern half of Rome's empire after the West fell to northern hordes. In the fifth century AD, a century after the West's collapse, Justinian faced riots in the Eastern Empire's capital, saw Northern Africa still overrun by the Vandals, and was pressed by the Persian Empire to the East. Despite not speaking the Eastern Roman Empire's default language, Greek, Justinian promulgated a new legal system, the Justinian Code, expanded the Eastern Empire, retook North Africa as well as Sicily and two thirds of Italy, and launched a period of Byzantine rule over the Aegean that would last some five hundred years, with the Eastern Empire lasting about a thousand years before falling to the Turks in the fifteenth century, its longevity fostered in part by Justinian having stamped out early schisms in the Eastern Orthodox religion.

Hanson notes that a big key to Justinian's success was that even though he got maximum publicity value out of new construction and military victories, he was actually quite stingy about such projects—using contractors and what we would now call special forces in his cautious overseas military operations.

Hanson sees a similar desire to boost national morale while also getting the biggest bang for your cautiously spent buck (or your *solidus*, in the case of the Byzantine Empire) in many great leaders of the past, including Pericles, Alexander the

Great, Justinian's predecessors Augustus and Constantine, the later Holy Roman Emperors Charlemagne and Joseph II, Queen Elizabeth I and Churchill of England, Catherine the Great of Russia, and Abraham Lincoln.

They were important not just because of military victories, argues Hanson. They shared a similar nationalist conviction: "They have a historical sense that decline is not a matter of exhaustion of natural resources, or it's not predicated on enemies over the next hill. Usually, it's internal."

That is, argues Hanson, troubled states in the past faced woes of their own making not so unlike our own: Their currency inflated and thus diminished in value, the treasury depleted, the military weakened yet overextended. What was needed, over and over again, was a changed "state of mind," he says. Great rulers saw that what was often needed was a dose of "reactionary nostalgia" and "a return to basic principles." The great leaders in those situations had an intuitive talent for getting people to "go back to first things" by force of personality, back to those things that made England or Russia or other lands succeed.

Many of those keys to success still apply to nations seeking restoration today. You have to have a balanced budget. You have to have sound money in the economy, beyond the manipulations of bureaucrats. You need transparency instead of corruption in government (or at least a willingness to treat corruption as the great common enemy so that it is constrained). In military matters, you need a sense of how earnestly to fight and what your endgame is.

The belief that the bad conditions are "inevitable" and unchangeable is a dangerous, self-fulfilling prophecy. We'd been told ISIS and the Paris Climate Agreement were inevitable—just as pre-Reagan America was told by Jimmy Carter that America needed to get over its "inordinate fear of communism" and accept the permanence of the Soviet Union. But these things aren't unchangeable. Believing that they are beatable can help make them so.

One must dare to believe greatness can come again.

CHAPTER 3

No More Accepting Decline

Trump's critics may not see in the MAGA Doctrine principles that span beyond Trump's own lifetime and beyond our own shores—but some people overseas do. Just as the United States was an inspiration to people resisting monarchies around the world at the time of the American Revolution and an inspiration to people resisting communist tyranny during the Cold War, the distinctive red Make America Great Again hats of Trump supporters have found their way to Hong Kong, during the 2019 protests there against some of the ways Beijing, back on the Chinese mainland, rules its less-communist "special administrative region."

Brave protestors wear Make Hong Kong Great Again hats—and borrow other American symbols, including the American flag. Confused, the American press unhelpfully

worries that bad elements, perhaps even white supremacists, may be infiltrating and exploiting the Hong Kong
protestors, though an East Asian protest movement is an
odd place to look for white supremacists.

The simplest explanation is that the protestors, like Soviet
teens listening to rock and roll on the sly decades earlier,
recognize symbols of Western-style freedom when they see
them. And they should: Hong Kong was by some measures
freer than the West when it was populated by refugees from
the mainland's communist rule for decades but not yet governed by the mainland (the United Kingdom handed it over
to Beijing in 1997 after a century and a half of colonial rule).
Let's hope its freedom and love of the free market endure any
crackdowns from Beijing.

Trump isn't up against domestic foes as totalitarian as the
Communists in Beijing, a few extremists notwithstanding,
but, like the Hong Kong protestors, he faces the daunting
task of transforming a stubborn, inflexible, corrupt, big-
government system.

One irony of our situation is that the American government got this bloated in part by fighting actual Communism
during the Cold War but hasn't seen much of a "peace divi-
dend" since then, despite the immense opportunity afforded
by the collapse of European Communism to reduce military spending. Ryan McMaken, senior editor at the think
tank the Mises Institute, notes that there has in fact been
an increase in defense spending of about 44% (adjusted for
inflation) since 1990, when the Cold War ended. In fact,
combined spending on the departments of Defense, Veterans
Affairs, and Homeland Security will reach nearly $1 trillion
in 2020, about a quarter of the entire federal budget.

How can peace be almost half again as expensive as decades of war? The truth is, peace is not expensive. Peace allows people to engage in commerce, to work and to build businesses without fear of violent disruptions. What we have now is a combination of relatively small-scale regional wars as in Afghanistan with low-level police actions—and the maintenance of expensive bases—all over the world.

When Trump resists constant calls for more military intervention around the world—when he says no to putting more troops in Syria and publicly contemplates pulling troops out of Afghanistan—he is not only pointing the way to peace but implicitly taking on a system of defense contractors and sometimes-opportunistic allies that has reshaped American thinking in a profoundly unhealthy way.

Republican senator Chuck Grassley of Iowa put it well in the *New York Times* when he wrote, "Over the past few months alone, the Defense Department has had to explain why it's been paying $14,000 for individual 3-D-printed toilet seat lids and purchasing cups for $1,280 each. These are just the latest examples on a long list of unacceptable purchases made by the department, including $436 for hammers in the 1980s, and $117 soap dish covers and $999 pliers in the 1990s."

Whereas once we thought of wars as things that begin and end, we have been lulled, for reasons of both profit and ideology, into assuming that war, like domestic policing, is effectively permanent. There will always be a terrorist somewhere, a "peacekeeping" mission, an authoritarian regime that might be better kept in check if we engaged in a big enough show of strength (formerly called saber-rattling, a quite honest metaphor).

The rationales for more military spending are always close at hand, often eagerly provided by the defense contractors who stand to get subsidies from increased military activity (and by the various think tanks and pundits closely allied with those defense interests). It has been a standard conservative talking point at least since the Vietnam War that American defense spending has been cut to the bone by the left—and the left has sometimes made reckless cuts. Yet the United States still spends about three times as much on defense as China, ten times as much on defense as Russia, and vastly more than any of its other rivals—or its allies, who end up depending on us. We spend about as much as the next seven nations combined, and instead of gaining peace we gain the vexing sense that we "ought" to be intervening in every conflict that we might in theory be able to nudge to a better conclusion, every regime we might in theory be able to topple in favor of a slightly better one—even if our track record suggests this is only occasionally so.

It's not that everything America does in the name of defense is evil or imperialist, but this is a system that has taken on a life of its own. If Making America Great Again means asking whether government spending is benefiting our nation, even the military defense of that nation must be open to critical scrutiny. At some point, waste becomes as toxic as hostile outside forces, and potentially provocative in itself. Military excursions that ought to make us think twice seem deceptively simple if the war planners have a trillion dollars to blow and the lives ended are not their own.

Recall that our 2003 entry into Iraq was caused in part by our conviction that any conflict with Saddam Hussein would be as easily won and as quickly resolved as the repulsion of his army from Kuwait in 1991. Sixteen years after the second Iraq War began, we're still picking up the pieces from that error in judgment. At some point the public has learned, but those in power haven't. When we try to impose our way of life on others it has seldom worked. In the Middle East, it has yielded few benefits for the United States. Can anyone argue that the Middle East is better off today than it was prior to 2003?

The MAGA Doctrine is not a threat to other nations but an invitation to deal with each other out of practical self-interest instead of ultimatums, displays of might, reckless adventures, and big crusades against small-bore enemies such as Afghan villagers or Latin American coca farmers.

However, that transition from a world of constant war—and constant big spending on domestic projects at home—will not happen overnight. There will be many small steps forward and occasional big lurches backward. I think President Trump is hinting at an end to the Afghan war, though some neoconservatives might not be happy about it.

America should not be sacrificed for a mission of global transformation that may or may not improve a few foreign regimes but will not easily redound to our benefit at home, and may in the long run create more conflict abroad by fueling resentment of our efforts.

After nineteen years of the war in Afghanistan, nearly 2,400 American soldiers are dead, and virtually no US citizen could say exactly what our goal in that country is now. The immediate goal in 2001 was to strike back against al-Qaeda camps in the wake of the 9/11 terrorist attacks, but that mission soon expanded to dislodging the Taliban government of Afghanistan that had sheltered al-Qaeda, then to eradicating

Taliban influence throughout that rural, rocky, and divided country even after we'd dislodged the government from the capital and gone to great lengths to create and stabilize a new government.

Even with that goal largely achieved, we keep some fourteen thousand troops in that country, risk further accusations of being erratic as we call and then cancel peace summits (as the president did in the fall of 2019), and delay the day when the Afghans must, inevitably, take full responsibility for their own peacekeeping. I would not blame President Trump for pulling all US troops out of Afghanistan even without another peace conference with the Taliban (which beats adding to the $3.6 trillion we've spent throughout the Middle East since the war there began). He is admirably fond of making good deals, but the best deal for Americans may be to get out of there. Most Americans know that.

The days when fragile American pride required that we fight every imaginable enemy to the end of days are, I think, fading into history along with duels and empires.

One reason the post–Cold War foreign policy consensus, shaped by a mixture of neoconservatives and "Scoop Jackson" (that is, hawkish) Democrats, had such staying power was the relative stability of the Cold War standoff itself. So long as the United States and USSR (or later even just the United States and the remnants of the USSR) appeared likely to stay in place for decades, the same or very similar experts could make the same foreign policy pronouncements year after year and sound as if their words were not only wise but timeless. The Cold War seemed as if it might last forever.

But just a few years before I was born, all that was over, and though no one was quite sure what would come next, the old policy experts were still in place. They still had their right-vs.-left panel discussion shows. They still had their think tanks. They still had their cozy relationships with politicians old enough to head prominent congressional committees. No one was going to budge in their thinking if they could help it. Strategic ideas about confronting rival superpowers such as China would just be mapped sloppily onto new threats such as al-Qaeda, and if anyone questioned the wisdom of confronting such a stealthy movement with old-fashioned, massive displays of military resources, their patriotism could always be questioned to shut them up.

North Korea is a perfect example of how hollow the old ways look when applied to new circumstances. The large, relatively stable Russian and American superpowers engaged, albeit in radically different ways, with a much broader world and had their respective reasons to take treaties seriously, at least much of the time. North Korea was a one-man dictatorship, nicknamed "the hermit kingdom," primarily interested in preventing almost any contact between its people and the outside world. Even limited trade with Japan might stir up curiosity in the North Korean people about an outside world they are forbidden to visit or exchange ideas with. North Korea would do or say anything to keep other nations off its back in the second half of the twentieth century until it could get back to doing the one thing that earns a nation truly hands-off treatment from the superpowers: building nuclear weapons.

This did not stop Bill Clinton from proudly proclaiming that an antinuclear accord with North Korea had been reached in the early 1990s, nor his secretary of state, Madeleine Albright, singing a jocular burlesque song at one international diplomatic conference about how North Korea used to be considered "rogue" (that is, it was on the official list of Rogue Nations) but now, having signed some papers with Bill Clinton, was "so vogue." Cause for laughter, no doubt—and North Korea was the one laughing, since it had no intention of honoring any meaningless paper antinuclear agreements.

If the average American had opined in the late '90s or the '00s that diplomacy with North Korea is pointless because they don't respect us and can't be trusted to tell us the truth, that American would have been declared an obstinate know-nothing. Maybe the experts, in this as in so many other areas, need to be taken down a notch, and someone like Trump who's willing to make a fresh start—and offer a dazzling vision of trade, hotels, movie-making, and new wealth to a newer, younger North Korean leader—is just what is needed.

Or as Don Jr. once put it, despite decades of experts and diplomats such as Albright calling the shots on North Korea, his four-year-old seemed to know about as much about how to deal with that nation as the purported experts. His four-year-old daughter had accomplished just as much as those career officials who had dedicated their entire life to engaging North Korea, and the result was zilch. Maybe someone willing to shove the piles of meaningless paper agreements aside and form a new, more personal bond with a rival leader is just the change in strategy that region needed.

Similarly, the USMCA, the United States–Mexico–Canada Agreement, hammered out by the Trump administration during his first few months in office, was initially described by the longtime supposed trade experts as if it would devastate North American trade and ruin decades of delicate work done by lawyers and politicians throughout the region who had crafted NAFTA, the North American Free Trade Agreement, in the 1990s and managed its implementation since. Trump's globalist critics were sure that he would smash the delicate web of commerce in his protectionist mania and, like a political neophyte, leave nothing in its place.

But USMCA, if ratified, will not just smash NAFTA. It refines it, making it easier for companies to share information across borders—and to seek redress for cross-border copyright violations—without some of NAFTA's burdensome reporting requirements that made governments privy to all the data used by international corporations. Instead of creating insurmountable trade barriers between nations, which was the greatest fear of free-market conservatives of the pre-Trump variety, USMCA would lower most tariffs and simplify trade quotas.

At the same time, it gently increases the pressure on any new south-of-the-border signatories to recognize the right to collective bargaining. Unions may not deserve special subsidies or regulatory privileges from government, but the days of them being stamped out by government, as was routinely the case in the United States a century ago and is sometimes still the case today in Latin America, should end. One result of the MAGA Doctrine has been to expose the left's incoherent policies, a product of hypocrisy at the highest levels of Democrat leadership. Think about it. For decades, Democrats complained about NAFTA, but it's President Trump who gets a deal that unions should applaud. You would think Democrats would be jumping up and down to pass legislation benefiting everyday Americans, but instead they have stalled the process, and as of this writing the treaty has not been ratified. Nancy Pelosi continually moves the goal posts, always declaring Trump's efforts insufficient.

The MAGA Doctrine aims for fairness and the rule of law, not just the pitting of one social stratum against another. It's no surprise, then, that President Trump has stalwart supporters in the upper echelons of business and among blue-collar workers. If ratified, USMCA will be win-win for all the trading partners involved. And in the end, it's all the individuals and companies engaged in trade, not the politicians who referee those trades, who matter.

The president must of course work in concert, and sometimes in conflict, with the two other branches of government, the judiciary and the legislature. But a president has a unique power to set the tone for future policy discussions, and I thus find it inspiring that President Trump has even dared to talk about restoring the gold standard.

We should not find that idea as shocking as we do these days. After all, the gold standard was the basis of the US dollar for over a century before Nixon abolished the last vestiges of that monetary order in the early 1970s. Gold is not some strange, alien substance. It's just a reliable store of value to which the value of a unit of paper currency can be pegged. By contrast, when those units of paper currency are not explicitly pegged to some such physical standard, they tend to end up being inflated willy-nilly—that is, more dollars are printed, making each less valuable (and prices likely to rise accordingly) without you even feeling the siphoning going on in your wallet. With good reason, a currency that gains and loses value at the whim of governments' central banks (with their printing presses) is called a "fiat currency."

Like most presidents, Trump has shown a reluctance to have the Fed tighten the money supply suddenly and risk cutting off a boom on his watch, especially in an election year, but one of his charms is his willingness to remind people, so to speak, to hate the game, not the player. Just as he admitted during the 2016 campaign that he had schmoozed politicians when he was in private business but recognized the corrupt nature of the whole political class, so, too, is he willing to nudge the Fed's interest rate decision-making timing in his favor while calling the whole system into question in a way few politicians would dare (with the notable exception of tireless critic of the Federal Reserve and defender of the gold standard Ron Paul).

The post–World War II financial order was a big move away from the objectivity and apolitical reliability of the gold standard, not coincidentally timed to coincide with the creation of powerful, intergovernmental financial agencies such as the International Monetary Fund and the World Bank, which are structured, not wholly by chance, as if to keep the world dependent on government loans from the major Western powers. The world resents the leash, and we should be letting the market, not bureaucrats, decide where wealth flows.

But the post–World War II order, launching as it did amid the efforts to rebuild nations ravaged by war, could always be spun as an economic order founded on "generosity." The generosity is often more than we can afford, though, and the allegiance it supposedly fosters in the wider world has been shaky. All the while, though, the bureaucrats themselves, and their elite close business allies, seem to prosper. Swiss bank accounts were meant to be a haven for capitalists, not a model for elite governance.

Just as Trump has had the audacity to question basic elements of military and fiscal policy, he has shown a willingness to make sweeping, pro-business regulatory changes. According to the Office of Information and Regulatory Affairs (OIRA), Trump's freeze on new regulations has saved the economy some $23 billion per fiscal year. By contrast, OIRA estimates that the Obama administration imposed $245 billion in regulatory costs in its first twenty-one months on the job (as recounted by the Brookings Institution). Donald Trump has always been a builder, from hotels to casinos to golf courses—Barack Obama was a community organizer who gave impressive speeches. However, one of the least eloquent points that President Obama made during a speech was his infamous line "You didn't build that." It's no surprise that President Trump understands that businesses and growth are good for the economy and create jobs, while President Obama focused on the government as the solution.

The precise numbers will be debated endlessly, but the difference in philosophical orientation is striking: The Democrats think they are "helping" America the more rules they impose upon us. Their philosophy of "from cradle to grave" has been slowly creeping into the daily psyche. The government will always be there for me and will know what is best, according to many on the left. Yet, that's not the motivating idea of America nor of our Founding Fathers. The less government exists, the more people are free and able to flourish.

Trump learned firsthand that new rules are a burden. And businesspeople don't just want to get rid of regulations to run amok and poison their customers, either: Dead customers won't make you much profit, their surviving relatives may sue, and such behavior will tend to make your insurance premiums go through the roof. Most regulation is redundant. As a product of the political process (its secretive, executive-agency parts, not even the out-in-the-open congressional debates we can all easily observe, which are authoritarian enough), not a product of market forces, regulation is not necessarily efficient. It just has to sound good in theory, or at least well-meaning.

Why have we for so long passively assumed regulatory bureaucrats know what constitutes good business behavior? Trump makes no such assumption. He is a skeptic, and his skepticism is directed at the powerful, not at those who suffer beneath the edicts of the powerful. He's on our side.

The failed Democratic presidential candidate Beto O'Rourke strikes me as a perfect illustration of how the left isn't just wrong in its notion of what laws and regulation can do—it's evasive. Take gun control as an example. Not only did O'Rourke scoff at the idea that Democrats want to take away people's guns, then say with pride during a primary candidates debate that he's coming to take away your AR-15, as if he's entitled to contradict himself at will, but like many Democrats, he doesn't seem very interested in keeping track of what's "voluntary" and what's mandatory.

He said he wants a massive national gun buyback to get guns "off the streets" (as if career criminals won't just buy new guns if they sell the old ones), then he says the gun buy-back will be mandatory (making one wonder how the "buy" price is to be established, but that's a comparatively minor detail), and then he predicts his mandatory buyback program will be complied with voluntarily. How convenient! That should avoid anything messy such as police battling to the death with reluctant gun owners who resist the edict. Everyone will naturally want to play along, and thus the legal penalties will be almost irrelevant.

I find this is how most Democrats, if pressed, think all regulation works: Their plans are so great that all but a few people will comply with them without even having to be threatened with fines or jail time. Of course, that makes me wonder why they still have to decree the fines, taxes, and jail time. Just for emphasis, I guess!

I don't think it occurs to the Democrats that every time they make new rules, decent people must now scramble to comply with those rules. It pleases me that some Trump appointees have spent more time issuing decrees to their agencies to do a better job of policing themselves internally than they've spent issuing new decrees for society at large to follow. Trump's Environmental Protection Agency head, for instance, ordered a drastic reduction in the use of testing on animals at that department. Good news for the animals. Better that than telling 330 million other Americans they have to perform six new tests before using pesticides in their backyard tomato gardens.

Democrats want to control your healthcare, your air travel, your vehicles, your light bulbs, your food, your straws, and your paycheck. It sometimes seems as if they want to tighten government control over everything in the world except the southern border of the United States (where, as I write this, illegal immigrants are literally creating contests to see who can get around or over the existing border wall the fastest, something that will be much harder to do if Trump is allowed to complete it).

They are eager to regulate and to censor, though they always seem to calculate how the regulating and censoring will affect their electoral prospects before taking action. I don't think they'll be too eager to rein in Google so long as that company and other social media giants lean anti-Trump, for instance. But nearly every other aspect of American life is regarded in the Democrats' eyes as improved by the loving touch of regulation.

Ironically, the left have tried to rebrand themselves as "progressives." The one thing they all seem to agree on is that America is in decline. We are losing cultural influence. We are no longer a moral beacon. Our workers are losing their jobs while Jeff Bezos gets insanely rich, and there is little anyone can do about it. Democrats are no longer optimistic about their country.

It takes a daring person, a larger-than-life person perhaps, to shrug aside those assumptions, to shrug aside the web of regulations, to shrug aside the guilt-tripping that the left so often now deploys as its main cultural weapon, and say, no, we're going to do things differently now. Trump appears to be such a person.

CHAPTER 4

America First

The MAGA Doctrine, far from urging belligerence against other nations, recommends recognizing the limitations of our knowledge of other cultures and thus refraining from trying to control them. The US government can barely run our own country, so it should be very cautious about trying to run others.

Take the ridiculous case of the Kabul Grand Hotel.

As NPR's Rebecca Hersher reported in 2016, some $85 million were spent by the US government and associated financing agencies to build a hotel in Kabul, the capital of war-torn Afghanistan, that was intended to be a showcase of America's rebuilding of that nation after having toppled its Taliban government in the previous decade.

If ever there were a project that had symbolic, rather than just practical, significance, this was it.

If ever there were a branch of the US government that is touted as having a tough-minded regard for making the difficult choices, being efficient, and avoiding rosy optimism, it is the US military, treated with understandable respect even by conservatives who look askance at all other government spending projects.

If ever there were a time when America was under pressure not to falter on the international stage, this was a project in a bright international spotlight, one that should not, could not, fail.

And if ever there were an easy location for our troops overseas to monitor, surely it was this hotel's location: directly across from the US embassy and easily watched from the embassy windows.

In 2009, US ambassador Karl Eikenberry told a crowd attending a celebration of the hotel project, "The development of this marquee American hotel brand sends a very real message that Afghanistan is open for business." As is so often the case with big construction projects, governmental or nongovernmental, the hotel was touted not just for its eventual usefulness in accommodating guests but its usefulness in creating jobs, in construction and other fields, in the interim.

This project would be a winner.

As a report from the Office of the Special Inspector General for Afghanistan Reconstruction detailed, the project soon went awry. As could be readily seen from the embassy, the "hotel" was but a shell, a few rooms completed for the sake of use in promotional photos—propaganda both for the local hotel-building company and for the general success of American intervention abroad—with the rest empty for years, even as the US taxpayer–funded coffers of the project emptied to who knows where.

As NPR's Hersher concluded:

> *The loans went primarily to a development company called Tayl Investors Group, which is incorporated in the British Virgin Islands and run by a Jordanian citizen named Fathi Taher. Taher and his US sponsors submitted the plans for both the hotel and apartments, and his company was the project manager for both buildings.*
>
> *As the projects got underway, OPIC [the US government-run Overseas Private Investment Corp.] relied on the Tayl group for updates on the hotel. For the apartment building, the agency hired a Bulgarian company, Gardiner & Theobald, to monitor progress.*
>
> *"Ironically," the report states, "Gardiner & Theobald never visited the apartment project site, and instead relied on information provided by the loan recipients to complete the status reports it provided to OPIC."*

To add insult to injury, as the *Financial Times* reported in November 2016, the hotel and an adjacent apartment building both ended up not only abandoned but constantly guarded by US security, since the abandoned shells' proximity to the US embassy would make them perfect staging areas for terrorist attacks on the embassy.

In short, US taxpayers spent tens of millions funding empty shells and then more money making sure they wouldn't be used to attack our embassy—and this is the sort of "marquee" project that our bravest and most self-sacrificing youth are fighting to make possible while they could be back home in the United States engaged in business or charity that would benefit Americans.

Pointing out the absurdity of this situation is no insult either to American troops or to the long-suffering people of Afghanistan. It is not a chauvinist, snarling insistence that Americans should flourish while distant foreigners suffer. It is a mature recognition that we—or at least government—cannot get things done just by wishing it were so. The market mechanisms that provide constant correction in normal businesses aren't there when projects are just sinkholes at the end of a giant torrent of government money. That's true no matter which government we're talking about, no matter which branch of government, and no matter where the sinkhole is located.

The problem is compounded, though, when we are arrogant enough to think our government can work miracles in distant foreign locations when it can barely deliver mail back home. The phony miracles that were the Kabul Grand and its partner apartment complex are best off demolished, as are the fantasies of playing global policeman and global hegemon that created them.

Senator Rand Paul of Kentucky sent one of his top staffers, and my friend, Sergio Gor, to visit the hotel in person in Kabul on a Senate oversight trip. At a subsequent Senate hearing organized by Senator Paul, on spending in Afghanistan, John Sopko, the special inspector general for Afghanistan reconstruction (SIGAR), testified his colleagues have seen "far too many instances of poor planning, sloppy execution, theft, corruption, and a lack of accountability. . . .

Some of the most egregious examples SIGAR has identified include [the Department of Defense's] purchase of nearly a half-billion dollars' worth of second-hand airplanes from Italy that were unusable and later sold as scrap; the construction of an Afghan security forces training facility that literally melted in the rain; numerous schools, clinics, roads, and other infrastructure built dangerously unsound and with little if any concern for the costs of supplying and sustaining them; and a failed $8.7 billion counter-narcotics effort in a country where poppy cultivation increased by 63% last year alone."

The waste on such projects is not small, sometimes dwarfing even the ridiculous Kabul Grand, such as a $750 million electrification project that, it was belatedly realized, placed electrical towers on land the US project organizers did not own, plus numerous embarrassments like the new Afghan Ministry of the Interior, costing $210 million, that had non-working air-conditioning and sprinkler systems. Or how about building a compressed natural gas filling station that cost the US taxpayer millions of dollars? Do you know anyone in the United States who drives a car operated on natural gas? I don't either. And I doubt many in Afghanistan, one of the poorest and least developed nations in the world, have the ability to purchase natural gas–operated cars, even if the US taxpayer is building brand-new facilities for natural gas fuel.

Out of sight is out of mind, and when you're spending other people's money, as the government always is, waste is never in view—not even when the Kabul Grand is just a few hundred yards away from the eyes of thousands of embassy personnel, mocking our pretense of being nation builders. The answer, as with domestic government boondoggles, is not to pour more money in and "this time get it right." The answer is to stay out of these quagmires in the first place.

Meanwhile, even important US roadways such as Times Square have potholes, and we slowly become inured to the occasional rural bridge collapse, with resulting driver deaths. Dare to suggest pulling out of foreign military engagements and focus on our own problems, though, and you may well end up called an "isolationist" by both major political parties—and then both those parties will go back to borrowing more money from China, adding to the over $1 trillion we already owe them.

Is that any way to keep the United States out from under foreign dominance? There's something completely upside down about the way we're conducting foreign affairs.

President Trump has been described by critics both as stubborn and, paradoxically, as having "no fixed views" and thus being too easily swayed by advisors—by whoever spoke to him last, as some naysayers put it. The resolution to this paradox, no real surprise to anyone who has watched him work in the private sector, is that he is always seeking the best advice. Sometimes he knows what needs to be done and how. The rest of the time he values the insights of a soldier who served in Afghanistan as highly as any PhD working in the State Department. If he's getting the same opinion from all his advisors, he may keep asking people until he hears some dissent, to understand what all the options are.

No matter how beautiful the speeches of diplomats might be, for instance, and no matter how pretty their words, Trump is still willing to turn around at the end of a meeting and ask someone else—a general, a trusted advisor, a low-level but competent local—"Is that really true?"

He breaks the spell of elite pretensions the way we'd all like to when we watch the elite bungling.

Before Trump, the left wanted to change the world through global institutions, and the right wanted to change it through military intervention. Now we know the real choice is between government bureaucracies and the soldiers we endanger for their goals.

To someone as determined as Trump is to get results that benefit the United States, it will be no consolation if trillions of dollars are lost in Iraq and Afghanistan—and we are talking about trillions over the long haul, not "just" the tens of millions lost on a project such as the Kabul Grand—but pretty speeches are given about hopes for a better tomorrow and a more unified world. Those speeches, and the posh events at which they tend to occur, are what most of the political class live for. The MAGA Doctrine leads to tangible results for the people who have to live with those results. It is rooted in the commonsense cost-benefit analysis intuitive to all businessmen and seemingly obvious to the average person—but completely alien to the way most politicians and government bureaucrats think.

Congress has even fought in recent decades to prevent simple cost-benefit analyses being a part of legislation. The thinking seems to be: If it's something that sounds worth doing, we'll do it even if it's a money-losing disaster that makes people worse off than they were before and leaves the United States as a whole poorer than it was before.

Trump knows that doesn't make sense. It pains him, and that may be the source of his aggressive tone. It's not hate. It's the frustration we all feel watching the government flounder or make things worse while it endlessly celebrates its own achievements. People can only stomach so much of that before they seek some way to rebel, and the 2016 election was one result.

People also sense, even if they are not philosophers and could not explain this intuition in lengthy manifestos that would impress the intelligentsia, that the closer decision-making is to home, the more likely you are to have some control over it. When Trump told his inauguration crowd, "From this day forward, a new vision will govern. . . . It's going to be only America first, America first," he was not vowing to attack other countries. He was not vowing to make the people of the world feel like hated outsiders, though there will always be some haters in a crowd. He was assuring the crowd—and they appreciated it—that America itself will decide its destiny, not distant foreign entities we cannot reasonably hope to monitor or control. It's an orientation rooted more in pragmatism—the decentralized nature of economic decision-making—than in flag-waving triumphalism.

And with the federal government over $22 trillion in debt, it's a shift in emphasis that can't come a moment too soon.

It is striking that it is not just the American left that dislikes Trump (though he has a few grudging fans on the left, too, a phenomenon we'll revisit later) but also some of the most supposedly prestigious international organizations: the architects of the Trans-Pacific Partnership, the experts of the World Health Organization (a group that once declared North Korea a model for healthcare), the UN, the diplomats behind the Paris Climate Agreement, and, of course, NATO (especially the deadbeats, who probably won't be too happy if a proposed resolution saying each NATO member must pay exactly one twenty-eighth of the organization's cost goes into effect, despite all their complaining about the current outsize role of the United States in the group).

The press and the sorts of politicians who curry favor with the international elite—the Clintons and Obamas but also the John Kerrys and Joe Bidens of the world—naturally see those international groups as a sort of higher authority, rendering the most objective judgment possible on the anomaly that is Trump. But Trump's nationalist impulse—in a way that is analogous to a libertarian's impulse to tell regulators to stay off his land—is to say, mind your own business, globalists. And America will mind its own business. You get better decisions that way.

Further, as Trump has repeatedly made clear, saying "America First" does not for a moment deny to, say, France the right to declare "France First" the basis of its decision-making, or Portugal the right to think "Portugal First." To a great extent, that's how countries already think and behave in the international arena. Try predicting their behavior with any other model and see how far it gets you.

The MAGA Doctrine in foreign policy is just based on the obvious principle that people manage their own affairs better than they manage other people's affairs, especially against those other people's will—and no matter how good the intentions behind the managing.

As with so many about-face complaints the left makes about Trump, contradicting whatever they said just days before

2016 in order to remain in opposition to whatever Trump says, it is very strange to see the modern left expressing so much concern about a US president not wanting to meddle in other countries' affairs, a president not wanting military action unless necessary (wanting, some insiders think, to get most troops out of Afghanistan in 2020 or so), a president not wanting a more belligerent NATO or more alienated Russia.

Weren't these basically the foreign policy hopes and dreams of the left for most of the past seventy years? Were they joking? I would hate to think that which party currently occupies the White House is really the only thing that determines what they praise and what they condemn.

But there is a deeper, less fickle impulse at work in Trump's critics—and not just on the left. There has been a "foreign policy consensus," most of the time, throughout those seventy years. It spans both the major parties' establishments, right and left, and can fairly be called centrist. It is not simply evil, but it arose in historical circumstances that no longer apply.

In short, the post–World War II international order, as seen from the perspective of the most powerful country on Earth, the United States, was really an order founded (at least in theory) on generosity. Europe had been decimated by the Nazis, and much of it was now oppressed by the Communists, and so a wealthy and intact United States had a unique opportunity both genuinely to help out its allies in their recovery and to cement their loyalty in the quiet, four-decade struggle against postwar Soviet Communism.

That means that those international institutions against which nationalists and populists now rebel, groups like the

International Monetary Fund and World Bank, were to a large degree US or at least Western creations—and aimed at staving off outright socialism, in much the same way Franklin Delano Roosevelt's New Deal economic planning was meant to prevent the adoption of outright socialism at a time when it was percolating throughout the world.

Just as FDR's big spending and regulations would over the years lead to a legacy of government bureaucracy, waste, and debt, the international institutions we helped create now foster an expectation of handouts, loans, entangling alliances with attendant (and risky) military responsibilities, and an array of international trade restrictions more ornate than Trump's focused tariff volleys.

This doesn't much bother the mostly rich and (de facto or sometimes literally) aristocratic people who drift between private-sector jobs like banking and public-sector jobs such as diplomacy, overseeing this deceptively calm world order. It's not run by outright socialists but often, on the contrary, by elite, superficially conservative figures such as members of the Romney, Rockefeller, or Bush families—and more recently, upstarts such as the Clintons, despite their 1960s peace-and-love roots. They all talk like entrepreneurs at times, which is how they sometimes win the allegiance of voters who like small business or who hope all non-communist politicians are patriots. But at the heights of international power, business acumen and innovation are treated as almost interchangeable with socialist programs and fiat currency (print all you like without regard to whether we actually have any gold or other valuables backing it and hope your relatives and colleagues will be among the first to get the resulting flood of loans).

The elite planners no doubt truly believe they are the ones looking at the big picture, rising above what they think of as the pettiness of nation-state and flag. But that carries immense risks for the common citizens who may end up having to live with the international elite's bungled economic plans, misdirected loans, and unnecessary, casually begun military interventions.

I'm glad we've got a president more worried about whether we're getting a raw deal than whether he'll look "good" (as the entrenched elite define it) on the international stage. I'm glad the MAGA Doctrine puts America first. Americans are a charitable people, we give, we raise funds, and we help all over the world. But for far too long we have been led by a flawed belief that we become stronger when we borrow money from China to give to places like Pakistan. How about we fix our own problems first before we decide to rebuild the entire world? It's one thing to support nations around the world when we have a surplus, but we don't—we have a deficit. Would you go take out a bank loan to give your neighbors funds to rebuild their driveway? Essentially, for several decades the United States has continued to borrow and spend wildly all across the world, despite the fact that we can't afford it and have forgotten to take care of our own backyard.

Putting America first certainly doesn't mean envisioning the United States vanishing from the world stage, either. It just means that the measure of the beneficial impact of the United States is not the degree of its immersion in international organizations and the socialist mind-set prevailing in many parts of the globe.

In fact, many of those most bothered by the America First sentiment seem, when pressed, not to be calling for "American leadership," despite their love of that phrase, but rather for American submersion or erasure. They don't really want us to lead any of those international organizations they revere. They want us to submit to them, to become more like them, to take our place as just one more country, perhaps like one from Continental Europe, with dashes of developing-world flair.

CHAPTER 5

Ending the Endless Wars

Might Donald Trump be remembered as the president who brought about world peace?

The media focus on his sometimes-belligerent tone as if that best captures the spirit of his presidency. But as he told the people of Poland in a speech in his first year in office, most of us share "hope for a future in which good conquers evil, and peace achieves victory over war."

In that speech, he described Poland and the United States as kindred nations, not because of ancestry or a love of war but because both nations had retained their independent spirits and pride even when beset by outside enemies—as Poland, suffering under both fascism and communism, surely has been. He paused in the speech to praise Lech Walesa, the hero whose leadership of the Solidarity union put pressure on the then-communist Polish government to hold free elections, starting the process by which European

Communism would unravel in the 1980s, freeing hundreds of millions of people.

As President Trump said in that same speech, he was there "not just to visit an old ally but to hold it up as an example for others who seek freedom and who wish to summon the courage and the will to defend our civilization." If that is what it means to stir up nationalist sentiment, the world could use more of it. This is not xenophobia or isolationism but the will to defend freedom. This has nothing to do with favoring hate-filled racial groups, which no matter how often we denounce them the left will be happy to connect to all nationalist impulses. I support America First. I have denounced and will continue to denounce racist groups who claim to be superior due to their race.

While his critics see nationalism and patriotism as mere tribal drumbeating—of the sort they too easily associate with warfare—Trump makes the connection between nationalism and liberty when he tells the Poles, "This is a nation more than one thousand years old. Your borders were erased for more than a century and only restored just one century ago. In 1920, in the Miracle on the Vistula, Poland stopped the Soviet army bent on European conquest. Then, nineteen years later, in 1939, you were invaded yet again, this time by Nazi Germany from the west and the Soviet Union from the east. That's trouble. That's tough."

That's Trump—appealing with ease to his audience's most heartfelt concerns, not to divide Poland from its neighbors but to emphasize its resistance to tyranny. Trump was joined onstage that day by veterans of the 1944 Warsaw Uprising, in which Polish resistance fighters fought off Nazi occupiers.

Despite Trump's critics making him out to be some sort of modern-day fascist or a vassal of Russia, Trump knows full well what the Warsaw Uprising represents to the Polish people—not just fighting against the Nazis but doing so without the aid of the Russians. The Soviet military was by then advancing on Nazi forces from the east, but it notoriously stopped its advance long enough to allow the Nazis to crush much of the Polish resistance, underground forces who the Soviets knew could later prove as much trouble to Russia as to Germany.

As Trump recounted in the speech, Poland would escape Nazi domination only to find itself subjugated for four decades by Russian communism—and he went on to urge Russia to end its support for present-day authoritarian regimes such as Iran's and Syria's and to avoid interfering in Ukraine. This is not the language of a man indifferent to global affairs. This is the language of a man who wants to see each nation free to solve its problems without being steamrollered by vast global empires.

The Poles present at that speech understood the implicit message: Leave the fate of your nation in the hands of large military alliances beyond your borders, and you may be abandoned—or subjugated. Better to maintain your independence.

We often talk about armed conflicts as though one man can lead a nation to war. In fact, it's usually a bunch of out-of-control bureaucracies forcing a nation into it. We now live in a world where our alliances are more likely to push us into war than to keep us out of one.

The MAGA Doctrine means trusting more of the world

to solve their own problems, without the American government thinking it is responsible for, or capable of, doing it.

For avoiding war, what sort of thanks does Trump get from his domestic political rivals? In an early 2019 presidential primary debate, Democrat senator Kamala Harris identified what she considered the "greatest national security threat to the United States—it's Donald Trump," dismissing his talks with North Korean leader Kim Jong-un as a mere "photo op."

This superficial reading of Trump's dealings with foreign leaders captures an important difference between the way Trump thinks and the way the political and foreign policy establishment thinks. Contrary to the impression Harris gives, it's mainstream liberal politicians such as former presidents Barack Obama and Bill Clinton who live for mere photo opportunities.

Whether they're announcing an ineffectual climate treaty in 2015 (which would not make a substantial change in the level of gases that may not even threaten us in the first place) or the early-1990s agreement with Kim Jong-un's predecessor Kim Jong-il to completely dismantle the North Korean nuclear program (which North Korea proceeded to ignore), elite politicians love to congregate together in fancy settings and pretend the whole world is unified in its sentiments. Are gala events for dozens of diplomats in settings such as Paris not, at least in part, photo ops? But these are the photo ops that keep elite politicians convinced they're shaping the fate of the world for the better, so they're considered acceptable—records of history rather than public relations fluff.

Trump's approach—not so unlike the frenetic phone-calling, hand-shaking, and deal-making he describes in books about his career as a real estate mogul—is to eschew gigantic group agreements that often as not amount to nothing in practical terms, instead dealing with world leaders one-on-one, with the intimacy that makes individual personalities and small cues part of the negotiating process. It's analogous to the difference between centralized planning and individualized service.

The approach is also based on Trump's assumption that getting along with the rest of the world is a good thing. He doesn't think you achieve that by spending decades advocating "regime change," which very often means war, all over the world. By contrast, many politicians on both sides of the aisle, whether commonly thought of as "neoconservatives" or "neoliberals," have been united in their advocacy of frequent military action. Ask yourself whether you can distinguish between the foreign policies of Hillary Clinton and the late John McCain. Both advocated toppling governments around the world. Both backed the Iraq War. Both were aghast at the election of Donald Trump, who had said for decades that wars are a terrible waste of lives and money.

Make no mistake: Trump knows a strong US military is a key to maintaining world peace, and he wants the United States to intervene in a decisive, strong fashion when it absolutely must. But his preference, unlike that of so many establishment figures in Washington, is for peace.

Is there more to diplomacy than showing up on time to assemble with two dozen other world leaders all working from the playbooks arranged for them by dozens of handlers and international lawyers, most likely yielding a rubber-stamped extension of whatever the previous agreement was? World leaders like to come back home with some front-page pictures reminding their voters that the world might fall apart without them. Instead of sacrificing our sovereignty for a photo op, Trump likes to have one-on-one meetings with people who can change the outcomes.

As CNN's Chris Cillizza acknowledged in a piece chronicling Trump's frequent use of the line "We'll see what happens," Trump likes to maintain flexibility in his political dealings similar to what he describes in *The Art of the Deal*: "I never get too attached to one deal or one approach . . . I always come up with at least a half dozen approaches to making it work because anything can happen, even to the best-laid plans."

We'll see what happens—not because the man doing the negotiating is chaotic or out of control but because he's watching for the best available opportunities, wanting the best outcome for America. (And the sheer number of political factors the president has to keep in mind in dealing with foreign leaders is a reminder that there would be far easier, more direct, more efficient ways for him to set up hotel or media deals for himself if, as the left sometimes absurdly alleges, his entire presidency were a self-interested exercise in enhancing his business credentials. Imagine how much he might make if he devoted eight years just to creating golf courses and restaurants in Continental Europe instead of trying to get member dues out of NATO.)

He recognized immediately upon taking office that he and America had been saddled with a dangerously bad deal on Iran by the Obama administration, which had been eager to appear to have struck a peace deal of any kind, no matter how flimsy the enforcement mechanisms, no matter how unrepentant and insulting the Iranian leaders remained, no matter how quickly Iran appeared to be ramping up to future nuclear weapons production, and no matter how much de facto bribe money had to be flown to Tehran to grease the wheels.

Ending the bogus Iran "antinuclear" deal did not, however, result in all channels of communication being cut off between the United States and Iran—as Trump's critics predicted not so much based on experience but based on their need to make the Obama plan seem essential in retrospect. Despite pressure from administration hawks and an understandably Iran-wary Israel, Trump reached out in mid-2019 to one of the most steadfast opponents of unnecessary military interventions abroad, Senator Rand Paul of Kentucky, as an informal ambassador. Others, such as Japanese Prime Minister Shinzo Abe, have traveled to Tehran and delivered messages in hopes of restarting negotiations. Trump, long known for constant daily phone calls to people of influence—including the media—likes to keep the channels of communication open at all times. Unlike so many before him, President Trump is willing to meet with anyone, without preconditions. Who can forget the dozens of impossible conditions that previous administrations demanded of hostile nations before even sitting down for a meeting? How can we improve relations or tone down hostilities if we can't even talk around a table? President Trump will talk.

We'll see what happens—and the range of positive possibilities multiplies when we're still engaged in diplomacy, not hunkered down back home giving lofty but arrogant speeches meant to prime a nation for war. Better a statesman who finds a way out of war than one who too eagerly relishes looking statesmanlike in war. Liberals should know that. They long claimed to understand it.

One of the great dangers of basing international relations on a few sketchy ideals—instead of getting to know the opposition in an up-close and personal manner—is that one may fail to perceive what it is your rival wants. See what makes him smile, what makes him perk up and look as if he sees a chance for mutually beneficial action. Don't just read the long manifestos cooked up by the international relations experts far from foreign capitals. Look for a chance to make deals—not just opportunities to please international organizations like the World Trade Organization or United Nations.

The core Trump foreign relations principle of national self-determination is not novel. It only appears so to people invested in the stagnant foreign policy establishment as it has existed for the past century, since President Woodrow Wilson's grandiose but failed schemes to make the world safe for democracy through World War I and the subsequent abortive establishment of a League of Nations.

Tragically, the United States has rarely known a year without some military conflict, large or small, and has shed blood and lost money involving itself in conflicts the world over since its founding over two hundred years ago. President Obama became the first in history to preside over a war every single day of his presidency. We did, however, establish a history early on of avoiding "entangling foreign alliances" (quite unlike the explicit promise of NATO to treat any attack on any member as an attack on all, a formula ripe for World War I–like quagmires).

Trump supporters use phrases such as "America First" to express our renewed interest in pursuing our actual national interest rather than just blundering into any overseas conflict in which we think we can give a small boost to an ally, an ideal, or an oil company. For using the slogan, we sometimes get condemned as "isolationists" or even fascist sympathizers in the style of some (by no means all but some) members of the World War II "America First" movement that hoped to keep the United States out of World War II.

But the avoidance of unnecessary wars—anti-interventionism—is not isolationism. On the contrary, in the absence of unnecessary wars, the United States can reach out to the world with tendrils of trade and culture. In the absence of war, we can form lasting and influential relationships instead of leaving behind bombed-out cities and the bodies of our heroic troops. Cultural, educational, tourist, and business engagements between the United States and others often create stronger bonds than overthrowing regimes in hopes of discovering a modern-day George Washington. So many wished and hoped for a George Washington–like figure to emerge in the Middle East after countless wars. Instead radical Islam stepped in and filled the void after we intervened and left.

Trump's desire to keep the United States out of unnecessary foreign wars—and to protect our sovereignty by protecting our borders—has an important precedent in the Monroe Doctrine, an idea easily forgotten by the present-day foreign policy establishment in its eagerness to reshape the globe.

America's fifth president, James Monroe, was elected in 1816, two hundred years before Trump, and he governed a nation that only a year earlier had completed another war with England, the War of 1812. During that conflict, in the summer of 1814, the nation's Capitol was set on fire by enemy troops. One could hardly ask for clearer evidence of the threat foreign empires and war could pose to national integrity.

But that was not the only potential imperial threat the Old World posed to the newborn republic in North America. While monarchies reasserted themselves in Continental Europe in the wake of Napoleon's defeat, the presence of Russia loomed in the form of that nation's 1821 assertion of sovereignty over much of what is now Alaska and the Pacific Northwest. By contrast, the nations of Latin America were on the brink of breaking free from the Spanish and Portuguese empires.

The United States, a fledgling democracy eager to avoid becoming a plaything of the Old World's tyrannies, saw an opportunity to stand with—and of course to influence, for good or ill—those fledgling Latin American republics and to tell Europe's monarchs and tsars very politely to "Keep Out." President Monroe did roughly that in his seventh State of the Union address in 1823, explaining to Congress that the United States had conveyed to both Russia and England its intention to make North and South America off-limits to any future colonization by outside powers:

In the wars of the European powers in matters relating to themselves we have never taken any part, nor does it comport with our policy to do so. It is only when our rights are invaded or seriously menaced that we resent injuries or make preparation for our defense. With the movements in this hemisphere we are of necessity more immediately connected, and by causes which must be obvious to all enlightened and impartial observers . . .

It is impossible that the allied powers should extend their political system to any portion of either continent [North or South America] without endangering our peace and happiness; nor can anyone believe that our southern brethren, if left to themselves, would adopt it of their own accord. It is equally impossible, therefore, that we should behold such interposition in any form with indifference. If we look to the comparative strength and resources of Spain and those new Governments, and their distance from each other, it must be obvious that she can never subdue them. It is still the true policy of the United States to leave the parties to themselves, in hope that other powers will pursue the same course.

Though the United States itself would proceed to meddle in South American affairs repeatedly, the principle that other world powers should not has stood the test of time, and the United States managed to stay out of world wars for nearly a century after Monroe's proclamation.

In a further reminder that dealing with other nations in a businesslike fashion can yield better results than warfare, the Monroe Doctrine reached its logical culmination with the peaceful purchase of the Russian territory that is now (oil-rich) Alaska in 1867, not so long ago in the grand historical scheme of things. Some of today's pundits probably have completely forgotten Russia controlled that region just over 150 years ago and would call for an investigation if they remembered it—yet there were pundits and members of Congress who derided the purchase as (Secretary of State William) Seward's Folly at the time, thinking the Alaskan wilderness would never even be worth the small amount Seward paid for it—about 120 million in today's dollars. Russia might control that part of the continent to this day if not for the nineteenth-century push to keep the New World free of the Old.

Arguably the two biggest, most seismic shifts in US foreign policy behavior since the Monroe Doctrine were the shift under Woodrow Wilson toward the United States playing global policeman (at ever-mounting expense to American taxpayers) and Trump, at long last, raising skeptical questions about that role. Hawkish and interventionist foreign policy is one area of tremendous bipartisan support in Congress. The Republican chairman and the Democrat ranking member on the House Foreign Relations Committee are hard to distinguish in their votes when it comes to funding aid abroad or intervening unnecessarily. Though President Trump has not as of this writing completely withdrawn US troops from any of the countries in which they were engaged during the Obama administration, he has moved in that direction in Afghanistan and other arenas and has not deployed troops to any additional theaters—despite the seemingly permanent foreign policy establishment's endless wish list of places where the United States should intervene, ostensibly to rescue them and all too often merely to throw our weight around without any clear resolution. Our footprint is significantly smaller under Trump in places such as Syria, Afghanistan, and Africa.

Americans don't shy from fights, even very difficult ones, if they are confident of the moral purpose of the fight and are given some assurance there is a realistic plan for victory. After Vietnam, they became more skeptical, but conservative, patriotic sentiments for three decades thereafter still inclined many Americans to think the more American military interventions, the better. Two decades of inconclusive fighting in Iraq and Afghanistan—and seeing the toll on our friends, relatives, and neighbors in the form of PTSD and lost limbs—has contributed to a change in that attitude among conservatives (even as some Democrats, numbed by a few decades of Clintonite assurances that American troops simply perform "humanitarian interventions" with the blessing of the "international community," have started sounding like hawks).

There is nothing unpatriotic about staying out of fights that do our nation no good, or ones that have no clear moral purpose. Far from all being "fair in love and war," one of the most moral principles ever added to the canon of Western thought is the concept of a "just war," given its most famous formulation by St. Augustine in the early fifth century. He wrote, "But, say they, the wise man will wage just wars . . . for if they were not just he would not wage them, and would therefore be delivered from all wars." (Rather than revere Augustine for his moral restraint, our era practically bans him as hate speech—Facebook took down one conservative's post of an Augustine quote saying "all men are hopeless" because they "sin." Sounds like a valuable reminder to me.)

In contrast to the warrior creeds of some ancient cultures, Augustine, like St. Thomas Aquinas after him, recognized that the goal of all moral military action should be peace. He did not want armies to roam the world looking for territory to seize or subtle social problems to rectify with clumsy weapons.

Compare that deeply moral impulse to worldviews displayed in recent decades by the leaders of either the Democratic Party or, before Trump, the Republican Party. While Trump works to avoid the flare-up of total war with Iran, Mitt Romney, regarded by many of the "Never Trump" establishment Republicans as a voice of moderation and respectability, vowed in the early stages of his failed 2012 presidential campaign to take "military action" against Iran to stop its nuclear program if elected—not merely if a crisis arose, simply if elected. A vote for Romney was in effect a vote for war.

Democrats such as Hillary Clinton offer no real alternative. She backed, among other interventions, the Iraq War, the Afghanistan surge in troops, and, notoriously, the toppling of Qaddafi's regime in Libya, leading to years of still-ongoing civil war—and horrible though we all agree Qaddafi was, Clinton and Obama are in no position to lecture people on statesmanship and (in Obama's case) accept a Nobel Peace Prize after bombing a relatively prosperous African nation into a place of terrorist gangs and slave auctions.

There is very little difference when it comes to matters of war-making between the "neoconservative" views of Romney-style Republicans and the "neoliberal" views of Clinton-style Democrats. Both follow in the risky footsteps of Woodrow Wilson, seeing the United States as an almost unerring remaker of a poor and undemocratic world, a giant that can bend the populations of whole nations to its will, for their own good and with little cost. We keep falling into that delusional view of America's role in the world and paying a terrible price for it.

And they call Donald Trump arrogant?

President Barack Obama and President George W. Bush both long supported the expansion of NATO, allowing small nation-states such as Albania, Croatia, and Macedonia to join. Under diplomatic pressure from the world and even some pressure from his foreign policy team, President Trump finally agreed to Montenegro joining the coalition. Yet his skepticism was publicly known. It is a nation so small that it has only about 2,400 troops and 13 naval vessels, but NATO is treaty-bound to defend any member nation that is under attack.

The possibility of a skirmish between Montenegro and one of its neighbors, including Russia, is all too real. The United States, like all NATO members, would be committed to getting involved militarily against Russia over Montenegro in the event of such a clash—over a nation that most Americans likely can't find on a map. By contrast, imagine if the United States were attacked by a large world power such as China. God help us if we have to rely on those 2,400 Montenegrin soldiers. Some deals are just bad for the United States, inherently unbalanced. Trump sees that.

In their distinctive ways, both Presidents George W. Bush and Barack Obama embodied the arrogance typical of the foreign policy thinking that preceded Trump, the inheritors of the establishment conservative and establishment liberal traditions, respectively. Each man wanted to improve America's standing in the world by the criteria of his own philosophy.

Unfortunately, to Bush that meant avenging every wrong occurring in the world, putting America's stamp on each conflict around the globe as if we could be judge, jury, and all too often executioner for each of the innumerable crimes being committed throughout the world—and hoping along the way that American-style democracy (and American corporate interests) would flourish in the wake of any resulting carnage.

Obama, no less idealistic, saw his presidency as an opportunity to burnish America's moral image in the eyes of the rest of the world, beginning with apologies to all those who had been touched by US or Western colonialism in past centuries. To Obama, we would triumph not through strength in the usual sense, but, in typical modern liberal style, by signaling our willingness to abase ourselves. We wouldn't just cut military spending—we'd treat international institutions (and trade agreements) as if for too long we'd failed to see their superiority to old-fashioned, parochial institutions such as the US Constitution and American capitalism.

Obama thinks apology is statesmanship, and Bush thinks looking for criminals to fight is. Trump admires strength and tough talk to a degree Obama probably considers uncouth, but he does not believe in using it as indiscriminately as the Bush clan traditionally has.

Trump, unlike virtually every political figure in Washington, is goal-oriented. He is not interested in just signaling his allegiance to some far-distant cause, such as turning the Arab world into modern liberal democracies, great though that would be. He asks himself whether becoming entangled in foreign conflicts, in negotiations or military deployments, will leave America stronger after he's gone. With too many military quagmires of the past several decades, he knows the answer is either a grim "no" or an endlessly debatable "maybe." Not good enough. America deserves better—especially the young troops fighting its battles (or worse, fighting other nations' battles).

It is unconscionable that for decades we've expected heroes maimed by American involvement in unresolved conflicts overseas, and the families of those killed in those fights, to accept "We tried" as the best assessment of what was achieved by the fighting. Surveys now show most American soldiers think our recent wars have been unproductive. Maybe they, away from the spin machines of the Washington policy establishment, know what they're talking about.

Trump did not sound erratic to me in a Fox News interview with Tucker Carlson, shortly after Trump was condemned by many of the usual foreign policy establishment voices—including ones who normally present themselves as advocates of peace—for not attacking Iran over a downed American unmanned drone. He sounded, refreshingly, like a rare politician capable of making commonsense moral judgments, specifically the final judgment about whether to direct retaliatory air power at Iran after hearing from his foreign policy and military advisors:

Before I sent them out, they had to give me everything I wanted to know by seven o'clock. They walked in, they gave me everything but they didn't tell me how many people would die. How many Iranians—I know a lot of Iranians from New York City, and they're great people. They're all great people. We're all great, right? Iranian or not.

I said, "How many people are going to die?" And they said, "At least 150." I said, so . . . they shot down an unmanned— not a brand-new exactly thing either, the drone—they shot it down, and we're going to now kill 150—or many more people, you never know. Once you start doing what we'd do or what they'd do, and nobody does it better than us, you don't know how many people are going to die.

So I said, "I don't like that. I don't like it." And I stopped it before. *We didn't send them out. You know, there was a little incorrect reporting . . . like we sent them out, and we pulled them.*

Trump thoughtfully weighs costs and benefits—moral costs as well as financial ones. Keep in mind that wars are expensive, and the US federal government is already an astonishing $22 trillion in debt. That's more than the entire US gross domestic product for a year, and Congress shows no interest in cutting spending. How many more wars would the hawks like to add to our tab?

For too long, conservatives not so different in some ways from Trump or from me had an unusual blind spot on the issue of war. In much the same way that liberals treat every domestic program they like as if cost is no object, conservatives of the past, conservatives in the Mitt Romney, Bush, or John McCain mold, have tended to think as if cost is no object once a sufficiently horrible enemy is identified. But cost should be part of our thinking, especially when we can't fully predict the outcome of a conflict. What sort of regime will replace the one we try to topple? How much blood will be spilled in the process? How long will we be fighting? How long will we be attempting to nation-build after the fighting stops, when we could be building in America?

Recall all those stories you've heard about the Pentagon paying $70 for a hammer. That's not just a side effect of war, as some liberals might like to pretend. It's the same unavoidable inefficiency that plagues every government agency, whether its mission is domestic or foreign. Whether we conservatives like it or not, all government agencies, even the ones we admire, function a little like socialist countries. Resources get wasted, bureaucracy expands, innovation is rare.

Imagine how that galls a man like Trump who knows that every penny matters—and that every penny government has comes from taxpayers, not any profit-generating activity run by the government itself. Trump hears those stories about $70 hammers and, instead of thinking, "The military is stupid," the way a Vietnam-era Democrat might, he thinks, "We have to drive a harder bargain. We have to make better deals." That's much easier to do in the cool, rational light of peace than in the fog of an unnecessary war.

President Dwight Eisenhower—no hippie but rather a hero of World War II—reduced military spending, and he famously warned the world about the fast-growing power of "the military-industrial complex." It's not just an idea paranoid leftists cooked up to bash American pride. That complex is one of many sources of government bloat.

Trump has admirably balanced criticism of some of the reckless military cuts Obama made with praise of the overall goal of cutting the defense budget. He'd like to do it, if he can do so without ever putting Americans in jeopardy as a result. One of the most direct ways to make cuts, of course—a more sweeping way than combing through budgets and bureaucracies—is to reduce the number of wars we're fighting. He resisted sending more troops and money into the quicksand of the complicated Syrian civil war, and, as he proudly told Carlson in that same interview, he pulled about half our troops out of Afghanistan (after two exhausting decades) and said he would like to remove our troops altogether.

Presidents frequently embrace foreign policy, since the power-hungry can find unlimited power there. Trump has wielded that power sparingly. Trump's goals are both peace and strength. He knows these things are made harder, not easier, to achieve if we're at odds simultaneously with Syria, Afghanistan, Yemen, Iran, Venezuela, North Korea, and some elements in our fickle ally Saudi Arabia. Less conflict is better, not a sign of weakness or inaction.

The press really ought to be grateful we have a president who seems to enjoy lobbing rhetorical bombs on Twitter more than he enjoys ordering men to lob real bombs. Yet the left-leaning press, ostensibly peaceniks, are so knee-jerk in their opposition to Trump, his desire to avoid a war is sufficient to make them support war. I had thought that only Obama had a personality influential enough to make liberals love war, but it appears Trump's personality has as great an effect on them—except if he's against it, they're in favor of it. Obama drones children and gets a Nobel. Trump balks in a very human way at the thought of killing Iranians like the ones he knows back in New York City—Muslim immigrants, mind you!—and the press tries to make him out to be a wimp.

The fickleness of the left is startling. Code Pink used to march on Washington, urging President Bush to end Middle Eastern wars. Where are they now that Trump is trying to do so? Where is Michael Moore? Where are the drunk, washed-up Hollywood stars who screamed, "Make love not war"? Why is the left now so silent when this president calls for less intervention? Why is the left missing in action when this president calls for an end to the wars in Afghanistan and Syria? If you have liberal friends, ask them if they support ending wars only under Democrat administrations.

Most Americans aren't falling for it, and I don't think any of them are sitting at home now regretting that they haven't been sent off to march into Tehran. The young in particular have seen the toll of protracted warfare on their peers. One of the strange side effects of improvements in battlefield medicine is that there are more wounded and maimed survivors left alive to tell their tales than in many past wars. War leaves lingering and visible effects on American communities, and increasingly, people on both sides of the political spectrum are willing to say there had better be a very, very good reason, not just the usual abstract speeches about democracy and freedom, for wading into more combat.

For the right, the protracted wars begun under Bush are an even bigger change than they have been for the left. The left always had an anti-war faction. The right is still waking up to the fact that the things it truly values—such as community and civility and commerce—get blown to pieces in war along with everything else. So does America's ability to focus on its own domestic problems. Trump knows his first duty is to this nation, not the ones he may or may not be able to refashion according to our liking overseas. The desire to remake foreign nations on the cheap is as unrealistic as the desire to manage the whole domestic economy through socialism, and we should resist both impulses.

But for many people, including more than a few elderly news editors, the right/left paradigm from the Vietnam War era still dominates. They keep thinking of the left as the lovers of peace even when they're making war, and they keep thinking that a conservative in the Oval Office means we're on the brink of a complete breakdown in international relations, perhaps followed by nuclear war. They can't admit we have one of the most peace-loving presidents in recent American history on our side now.

This is a president who pursues peace not as if it were a hazy dream on the horizon, something to which we pay lip service while quietly sending in military "advisors" to lay the groundwork for larger later military deployments, but something achievable in concrete, piecemeal fashion the way business deals and nation-by-nation trade agreements are. Think of the specificity of the implicit deal he presented to North Korea's Kim Jong-un: Stop behaving like a rogue who lobs missiles at Japan, and you could be seen as the leader who brought your people peace and brought them normalized trade with the outside world.

Of *course* it was in part an appeal to Kim Jong-un's vanity—it would be insane not to appeal to vanity when you're negotiating with an unchecked dictator. Trump knows that, despite the shameful and disingenuous efforts by the American press to depict Trump as a genuine, naïve fan of Kim (or any other foreign dictator). While the press dreams of going through the usual empty motions—Bill Clinton's worthless paper agreement with the prior Kim, Obama's poetic assurances of an eventual better future—Trump sets specific goals and sizes up the person with whom he's dealing, dangerous or not, to figure out how to get the result best for the United States. He decides what his criteria for success are, and in a far more concrete fashion than most of the world's windbag leaders, he meets them.

Better that than the sort of sleepy march to world government you see happening in the European Union or the United Nations, all talk and no results except more bureaucracy. A nationalist leader who loves his country can make wise decisions on its behalf—and even love his ostensible enemies overseas as the fellow human beings they are. The cold-blooded international (and domestic) bureaucracies in which we've been asked to put our trust for the past several decades, by contrast, seem somehow to keep spilling blood all over the globe. They call it peacekeeping instead of war. Time for a new approach.

CHAPTER 6

Making the Economy Work Again

The Dow Jones Industrial Average is up about 9,000 points since President Trump was elected, as I write these words two and a half years into his first term.

Just a few weeks ago, at the July 2019 Turning Point USA conference I organized in D.C., President Trump, speaking to the crowd of conservative activist teens in attendance, said, as he has many times, that "sixty thousand factories and plants" have closed in the United States in the twenty-first century. Interestingly, though he attributed part of that loss to "dumb trade deals," he hinted at a solution other than imposing higher tariffs—a solution that probably goes a long way toward explaining the outburst of optimism among traders and businesspeople when he won the 2016 election.

He alluded to the improved tax and regulatory environment he is fighting to give the United States. One of his first actions upon taking office was to declare a de facto freeze on new regulations, also urging the executive branch regulatory agencies to repeal more regulations than they create.

Since the MAGA Doctrine is looking out for the little guy, Trump saw that this wasn't about the rich versus the poor. It was about individual workers and entrepreneurs up against regulatory bureaucracies and international trade agreements.

Liberals like to pretend that every regulation is a safety-conscious rule against poisoning customers or crushing workers with machinery, but most regulations do nothing to enhance safety that wouldn't be done by firms' own desire to keep their insurance premiums low (not smart to kill workers and customers if you don't want to get sued), and regulators add layers of needlessly rigid procedure, often merely because those procedures were the standard ones for industry leaders in years past—not a good way to create innovation through competition.

As Trump said in his TPUSA speech, those sixty thousand factories "didn't cease to exist. They moved to places that are easier to operate." In the long run, Trump doesn't want to wall off the United States from trade—far from it. He wants to make the United States once more the kind of place where it's easy and profitable to trade, and you make it that way in part through streamlining such as his tax reforms and his regulatory relief. He mainly deploys tariffs as one weapon that can be used to get rid of regulatory and tax obstacles US firms face from foreign governments when they try to engage in commerce overseas. (And even full-fledged free-traders like two of my heroes, economists Ludwig von Mises and Milton Friedman, have noted that if one must have a government, it is arguably better, and slightly less disruptive to commerce, to fund it with a tariff on imports, partly paid by people outside the United States, than with numerous internal taxes.)

Trump has been tough in his remarks about unfair behavior by China—violating US intellectual property, engaging in industrial espionage, using its military to subsidize many of its industries, pressing prisoners into factory labor—but he said in his TPUSA speech, "I don't blame China." He didn't mean he forgives their unfair or inhumane practices, but he understands their natural, nationalistic desire to make their own country richer by whatever means they think will work. "We should have done that," he added—meaning pass laws for a change that make it easier, not harder, to do business in the United States.

The Democrats have for decades approached regulatory decision-making—and the imposition of high corporate tax rates—as if businesses can overcome any obstacles government creates for them. They assume that there is no burden business can't carry, and that none will go looking for opportunities where the burdens are lighter. Then, when companies flee overseas, they whine about the outsourcing and offshoring they helped cause. To Make America Great Again, one obvious thing to do—obvious to anyone other than a leftist ideologue—is to make America hospitable to business again.

Judging by some of the basic economic facts about America during the Trump presidency, that's happening. Over 150 million Americans are now employed, the most people who've ever worked in this country, for starters. That's 150 million

Americans less likely to become dependents of the government, more likely to shape their destinies and live their lives.

And as the president observed in his TPUSA speech, he's achieved other things that for a long time we just thought couldn't be done—things we'd almost given up on as too politically volatile. ANWR, the Arctic National Wildlife Refuge—for years a green-politics hot potato—is now open for drilling (using pipelines safely distant from almost any ecologically significant land), one of several factors making the United States a net exporter of oil after decades of being dependent on the vicissitudes of Middle Eastern politics for our supply.

The media noticed such achievements, said Trump. "And their reaction? Impeach!"

Again and again, policies that would have been treated by liberals as commonsensical decades ago—or even immediately prior to Trump winning the 2016 election!—are now depicted as causes for outrage.

As Trump went on to say in his speech, liberals, including former president Bill Clinton, used to say, "It's the economy, stupid" when explaining political priorities. But once the economy starts booming under Trump, we stop hearing the media talk about it.

They used to say what matters is "jobs, jobs, jobs," recalled Trump. Yet when unemployment stats drop to historic lows, including for minority groups too often untouched by the broader prosperity of America, suddenly the media lose their long-time interest in tracking day-to-day unemployment percentages. "They drop that once we win on it," as Trump said. They turn their attention elsewhere, looking for ways to discredit the effort to Make America Great Again and denying we've begun to make the economy work again.

In a reminder that Trump is not, as is so often alleged, motivated by xenophobia in his policy recommendations, he also noted in his speech that the European Union is "worse than China" on trade. It's bureaucracy and red tape that he hates, not a short list of foreign foes, and he has begun working out better trade terms with China. Trump's foreign policy toughness ends up affecting our domestic economy in a good way, too. His historically unprecedented success in getting our European allies in NATO to cough up an additional $100 billion in defense spending shows what a leader can do when he refuses to pick up the check for every nation except our own. His penchant for tough deal-making in his private-sector life pays off big for the US public sector (and all of us who pay taxes to support that public sector).

Trump is not out to antagonize Europe or make that a continent of enemies. However, getting them to pay up—instead of letting the United States carry nearly the whole load of the NATO military alliance's expenditures—is one important way of showing we're putting America's interests first for a change instead of letting Europe slowly bleed us of funds while more hostile nations literally drain our blood.

"Somebody said President Obama is much more popular in Germany than President Trump—he should be," added Trump in his TPUSA speech. "If I start getting higher poll numbers in Europe, I'm doing something wrong." Trump was elected to govern the United States—and to govern for the United States—not to cater to a disapproving international audience that doesn't always share our values.

Trump sees that these issues—sound economics and a nationalist foreign policy orientation—go together for reasons much more logical than knee-jerk opposition to all interaction with foreigners. His instinctual wariness of deadbeats and moochers leads him to be skeptical of both Europe's socialist redistributionist tendencies in economics and its post–World War II tendency to let the United States carry most of the military defense load.

In the current relatively peaceful climate, why not let Western Europe have a little more control over its strategic destiny while also paying for that destiny like responsible adults? We have domestic priorities in need of attention, and we don't need to indirectly subsidize the welfare system of other prosperous states.

As Trump put it in that same speech to TPUSA, the Democrats like to pretend they understand Europe better than he does, but as usual, they opt to "understand" only the left-leaning, socialistic aspects of what they study. They point to Europe as a beacon of sophistication when its elites are on the same page as our left-liberal elites, wanting to tax more and regulate more. When Europe starts drifting away from that half-century-long pattern of "social democracy" (basically vast welfare states)—when populists win elections in Italy or Hungary or the United Kingdom and make the social-democratic consensus look more fragile—suddenly Europe isn't seen as so sophisticated by our elites. Suddenly it's described as too white, too old-fashioned, too unstable, or frighteningly populist.

Trump said in his speech that when you behold the initial batch of 2020 Democratic presidential candidates, "there's not a Winston Churchill among them." That is, no leaders who are willing to fight when necessary, make peace just as vigorously, and always remain on guard against those who, while sounding soft and gentle, would turn all our resources and decision-making power over to the state. "Socialism is not as easily defeated as you think," warned Trump after some obligatory jibes about young left-wing Democrats such as Alexandria Ocasio-Cortez.

He says he worries about the maintenance of the American entrepreneurial spirit that made us the ultimate capitalist success story "when I'm up there [on the debate stage] with some maniac" offering "free" handouts of every kind (in reality wasteful government projects supported by bilked taxpayers) to everyone, even illegal aliens—that stunning last wrinkle a topic for a later chapter and a new point of firm agreement amongst the "generous" Democrats.

But then, an uncritical unanimity in thought and collectivism in economics seem to go together quite naturally. Or, as Trump told the TPUSA crowd, "Socialism cannot survive when people are free to think for themselves, and America will never be a socialist country."

Though the Democrats have lately abandoned any embarrassment they used to feel about being labeled socialists—and now treat that failed philosophy of central planning as if it is the exciting future of their party—the undeniable historical fact is that the United States became rich enough to entertain

such juvenile economic fantasies by being the least social-
ist large country in the world. Consider what happens when
America's one large experimental socialist zone, the state of
California, goes its own way:

- California has 12% of America's population
- Yet they have 50% of America's homeless population
- And who has run and represented California for
  decades? People like:
  - Nancy Pelosi
  - Dianne Feinstein
  - Maxine Waters
  - Kamala Harris
  - Eric Swalwell
  - Gavin Newsom

Democrats in the Obama era didn't do much to spur economic growth but prided themselves on an endless variety
of redistributive mechanisms. From green energy subsidies
to encouraging the Federal Reserve's "quantitative easing"
as a euphemism for money-printing (and the resulting low
interest rates that hurt people who save their money), from
Medicare and food stamp expansions to keeping people on
unemployment for years, the Bush-era Republicans were
happy to play along with anything as long as it came with
bailouts for their fat-cat cronies on Wall Street after the 2008
crash.

Trump intuitively understands that you do not Make America Great Again by arguing over who gets the handouts, the
perpetually poor or the well-connected-but-undeserving.
There will never be enough government largesse, magically

conjured from the wallets of other members of the population, to spark greatness and inspire creators, only enough to salve wounds and keep people dependent.

Trump famously began his 2016 presidential campaign with the seemingly pessimistic declaration that "the American dream is dead." He did not mean, though, that the American dream *should* be dead. He meant that unless we changed course, moving away from endless debt, endless wars, and spending without regard to consequences, our house of cards would come crashing down. By contrast, it is the left that so often declares the American dream, even when achievable, a veiled nightmare.

Those Republicans who are guided by the MAGA Doctrine—of putting America first and once more encouraging all its citizens to flourish while standing on their own two feet—know that the real testament to a flourishing economy is not how many new government handouts we are offering (like the dizzying array of medical and other giveaways touted by the 2020 Democratic candidates for president) but *how few* people need such handouts. Wouldn't it be truly great if no one needed the assistance of government? Never forget that the more people getting government benefits, the greater the number of likely Democrat voters.

President Trump has moved some five million people off of food stamps—by helping to free up the economy and create more jobs, not just by cruelly kicking the former recipients out onto the street to starve. Where was the reporting on that beautiful accomplishment in the press that is supposedly run by reporters so concerned for the worst-off? After sixteen years where President Bush added eleven million people to the SNAP program (the official term for food stamps) and then Obama added sixteen million more, we finally have a president who has gotten over five million people off food stamps. How many reporters obsessed with the hardships of everyday Americans touted that achievement?

Although the Democrats can outdo "country club" Republicans on shoveling government subsidy money to cronies in industry—through sweetheart contracts, no-show jobs, and special tax breaks—there are times there is only one "business" they really trust to get bigger and bigger: *government*.

Trump, by contrast, arguably got his start in politics by tackling a very local New York City problem: the complete failure of that Democrat-dominated town to maintain the potentially lovely Wollman skating rink in famous Central Park. Despite the fact that anything as prominent as that often-visited park's skating rink should have been a point of pride for the city, the cracked and disused rink had languished ignored and in need of repair from 1980 to 1986, when Trump, then just a private citizen but one used to getting things built—and getting things done—offered to repair the rink partly at his own expense, within six months.

It was finished two months ahead of schedule and $750,000 under budget.

Think of the MAGA Doctrine as a simple code for turning that sort of practical problem-solving into a can-do approach to national governance. It's not about Trump bossing people around like a tyrant—it's about him demolishing obstacles so that the rest of us are free to rebuild. And even to skate.

CHAPTER 7

No More
Low-Energy Nation

In 1990 to 1991, two years before I was born, America fought what is now sometimes referred to as "the first Gulf War" in Iraq, to repel Iraqi ruler Saddam Hussein's invasion of neighboring Kuwait. That war lasted only seven months and claimed only 146 American lives (about a third of all allied deaths), or so it seemed at the time.

The resulting political and military tensions in the region would erupt again periodically for three decades, most notably in the far more protracted Iraq War that the United States started in early 2003 (after several years of occasional punitive bombing raids on Iraq) and the Iraq portion of the sprawling war a decade later against the terrorist group ISIS and its affiliates.

In Iraq alone, the United States had suffered over four

thousand deaths and thirty-two thousand injuries by the time Trump took office. As Trump lamented during his 2016 presidential campaign, the United States has now, in Iraq, Afghanistan, and the surrounding regions, spent some $6 trillion waging war since 2001, largely as a reaction to the September 11, 2001, terrorist attacks by al-Qaeda, which controls neither Iraq nor Afghanistan.

That $6 trillion is roughly equal to a quarter of the entire federal debt.

And throughout those wars, and ever since I was born, I heard the refrain, usually from protestors on the left, that the United States should spill "no blood for oil." It sometimes seemed like just another anti-corporate, Marxist taunt. But the more lives and money we expend fighting over regions that likely wouldn't matter to us so much if they had no oil—and which surely wouldn't have as much money to spend arming their local terrorist groups if they didn't have such a large share of the world's oil—the more sense the anti-war refrain makes.

The MAGA Doctrine means defending our soldiers and the average Joe filling up his gas tank instead of putting them in harm's way, no matter what the big oil companies, radical environmental groups, or Middle Eastern despots want.

Part of the answer, of course, is to change our military strategy, our understanding of our responsibilities to military allies, and our inflated conception of the ease with which other nations' cultures can be remolded and their regimes replaced. But another part of the answer is, conservatives have to admit, about oil production. The temptation to go to war decreases if oil becomes significantly more plentiful, less necessary for energy production, and more readily found right here at home without having to worry about the stability of regimes on other continents.

Less than a half-century ago, the Arab oil cartel called OPEC nearly brought America to its knees by temporarily reducing oil production—leading to the so-called energy crisis of the 1970s and the protracted economic slowdown that helped end Jimmy Carter's presidency and put Ronald Reagan in office.

Now, a combination of fracking, more precise drilling, and more efficient use of natural gas and coal are helping to make the United States nearly "energy independent," a stated but seemingly unachievable goal of every president since Nixon. It looked like an impossible dream for decades, something akin to "zero carbon emissions." But now the dream is in sight, in part thanks to Republican insistence on pursuing "all of the above" energy strategies.

Hillary Clinton predicted that under her administration, "We're gonna put a lot of coal miners and coal companies outta business." Instead, President Trump drilled (quite carefully and safely) in the Arctic National Wildlife Refuge, exited the Paris Climate Agreement, ended the Obama administration's regulatory "war on coal," and approved for use several oil and gas pipelines that had languished in environmental-regulation red tape.

Trump's reduction and streamlining of regulations and permitting procedures has helped push oil and natural gas production to record highs not seen since before the 1970s crisis (and the ensuing explosion in regulation). The United States doubled crude oil exports in 2018 and is a net exporter of natural gas for the first time in sixty years (exports to the European Union have nearly tripled).

All of this means an economic boon for the United States, but there is also an immense, more long-term political boon: The less dependent we are on the political stability of foreign regimes for our energy needs, the harder it becomes for military interventionists to justify risky military engagement abroad. That's a heartbreaking side effect for a few relentless hawks who, in their own perversely patriotic way, think that the more the United States meddles abroad, the better for everyone. It would be nice if it were that simple, but the body count and unpaid bills suggest otherwise.

When Trump says we are living in a "golden age of American energy dominance," he's not announcing a triumphalist oil-wars regime like that in the mad dreams of some of the neoconservatives. He's announcing the foundation for a new century of peace.

The left hasn't been without its energy plans, of course.

There's the Green New Deal touted by Democratic socialist Representative Alexandria Ocasio-Cortez, intended to effect in a few short years the complete transformation of civilization into one characterized by central industrial and economic planning, full employment but drastically reduced plane flights, and the adoption of delusional "modern monetary theory" under which no amount of government spending matters because the printing of new currency just crowds out old, pre-green activities in favor of all the wonderful new government-directed green ones.

Notoriously, after months of praising the plan, Senate Democrats voted "present" on the Green New Deal when given a chance to reveal where they stood on the proposal, with Republicans overwhelmingly opposing it and the whole deal going down to a stunning 57–0 defeat. The deal's pragmatist inspiration, President Franklin Delano Roosevelt, would have shifted quickly to another tactic, and the Democrats probably will, too, if only to avoid having to talk about the debacle again.

Some would-be Democratic presidential nominees have plans of their own as asinine as the Green New Deal, though. Bernie Sanders's plan would spend a stunning $16 trillion to nationalize large parts of the energy-production economy into something he describes as akin to a giant Tennessee Valley Authority. I mean, I guess it's better he's taken inspiration from that than from Stalin's Five Year Plans, but I wouldn't trust the government to do more with less under any circumstances. Nationalizing a big chunk of the economy probably means making it dirtier, less productive, and more expensive. "If you like your electricity, you can keep it." No thanks.

Most left-wing energy plans for a long time now, starting during that '70s crisis and accelerating during the big environmentalism fad of the '90s, have mainly focused on convincing Americans to use less energy. Their assumption—driven in part by an excessive fear of global warming—is always that we should be cutting back use, not increasing production. It's a stealth-Luddite agenda that implies humanity and all its activity is making things worse, is sinful in a sense, and ideally should stop altogether.

Former vice president Al Gore's climate change plan, touted in part through his film *An Inconvenient Truth*, would involve cutting human energy use by about one fourth, not the sort of thing you achieve just by doing a little extra weather-stripping around drafty windows. That'd be a big, sudden decrease in civilization's output and activity, likely yielding very little change in the Earth's (mostly naturally) ever-fluctuating temperature.

Despite all the efforts to terrify us about global warming, by the way, the fact remains that the Earth's temperature, to the extent it can even be reliably measured, has gone up only about one degree Celsius over the past hundred years, and sea levels have risen about three inches, which appears to be about the same amount they rose the previous century despite increasing industrial activity since then—and in any case, leaving people plenty of time to move a few inches farther away from the shore if necessary.

The Obamas don't seem too worried about the problem now that they're out of the White House and in mid-2019 bought a $15 million mansion right on the edge of a very flat stretch of Martha's Vineyard beachfront.

If the left sometimes show their hypocrisy and indifference to the masses on the energy and climate issue by doing things like flying private jets all the time or living right next to oceans they claim will rise to kill us all any minute, we should not become complacent about hypocrisy on the right, either.

The willingness of, for example, generations of the elite to fight those devastating wars over oil-rich regions is a perverse side effect of the mingling of private interests and public power. Just as government subsidies for pharmaceutical purchases start looking like a great idea if your family is in the pharmaceutical industry (or, like Medicare Part D architect and former senate majority leader Bill Frist, the hospital management industry), your family being in the oil business just might make you more willing, on a subconscious level, to tolerate great sacrifices (on the part of others, including taxpayers) in the name of keeping the black lifeblood of industry flowing.

It's not so crazy—it just isn't necessarily as objective an accounting of the costs as would be made in a pure free market, where you had to pay for the land where pipelines sit with your own money, defend pipelines in trouble spots with your own gun, and fight foreign dictators with your own mercenary army. If you're willing to do all that—without violating human rights in those countries—more power to you, no pun intended.

President Trump embraces ideas advanced by Senator Rand Paul of Kentucky, who has been equally skeptical of our so-called alliances in the Middle East. The more energy-dominant we become, the more we produce in forms ranging from oil to coal to hydroelectric, the less oil we have to buy from countries like Saudi Arabia (let us not forget fifteen out of nineteen of the 9/11 hijackers were Saudi Arabian) and Iran, which promotes terror throughout the Middle East and vows to bring about the destruction of Israel and America.

The philosophy of America First means that we no longer have to look outside our shores to fuel our ambitions or make strategic decisions.

The more we can steer clear of the trouble spots of the Arab world, the better, at least until such time as it has become a bit more tolerant and politically open. Having to recognize the United States as an energy exporter instead of importer might give some in that region just the dash of humility necessary in any culture, including our own, to foster civility.

In the long run, the best thing the United States may have going for it in a world desperate for steady energy supplies—so desperate it is sometimes willing to kill and be killed—is a culture of technological innovation. A few decades ago, virtually no one was writing about extracting oil from shale rocks or natural gas via fracking. Now the debate is often over whether these methods are too effective and have (minor) environmental side effects we dislike. So quickly we forget the old problems, like being at the mercy of the Middle East for our energy needs, and move on to more rarefied, relatively pleasant concerns.

Technological advances and growing wealth are like that. Long may they increase. I for one would take more pride in the United States coming up with whole new methods of producing energy—whether from oil, fusion, clean coal, or other methods we haven't even imagined yet—than in teaching a rising generation it needs to stop using light bulbs and driving cars.

Industry uses energy and ever-advancing technology, and that's something to be proud of, the hallmark of our species, not a sign of shame.

CHAPTER 8

America Is Not a Mistake

Imagine the world without America.

If you think America isn't so "great," with all its materialism and individualism, take a moment to consider what most of human history was like before the relatively recent eruption of America onto the scene. Two and a half centuries is just a blip in the grand scheme of time, after all. What was life like before?

Civilization as we know it has existed for only about twelve thousand years, with humans roaming in bands before that, searching for plants and prey to eat but not yet building farms and cities.

Then, for thousands of years, as cities grew into empires and culture became more complex, most people took it for granted that their lives would be run by tyrants—kings, emperors, Genghis Khan, maybe if you were lucky wise village elders who knew you well enough to show some mercy in their edicts about what you could say, do, hunt, draw, think.

Wars, though less likely to annihilate the planet than today's wars, were frequent and largely amoral. Your tribe raided the next village over because it could. Captives might be taken and enslaved. There was little talk of human rights or constitutions in the distant past.

An early death was the norm, with most children dying before they reached puberty, the average adult probably living to about the age of forty, and medical options very limited.

Over those millennia, virtually no human beings were lucky enough to accumulate wealth. That was for kings. Subsistence-level farming—growing just enough so that your family could survive (if you were lucky and worked from dawn to dusk)—was the norm, as some environmentalists in our day wish it still were.

America became the land to which people from the Old World could flee to ply their trades without answering to guilds, farm land without answering to the lord of the manor, pray without permission from the government's bishops, and talk about the affairs of the day without fearing reprisals from the king.

By no means were things fair from the outset in the eighteenth century, but the model of individual freedom that at first was applied only to white males was later expanded to women and ethnic minorities, to the benefit of all. That—not ditching the whole enterprise of American freedom—was the right thing to do.

Today, not only are there more Americans employed than ever before, but black unemployment is at historic lows, about 5%, and Latino unemployment hit a record low of

about 4% in April 2019. It is amazing that this has happened
on the watch of a president condemned as racist and anti-
Latino by the entire liberal establishment (one of the leading
2020 Democratic presidential candidates, Elizabeth Warren,
tweeted an unqualified "yes" to the question of whether
President Trump is a "white supremacist").

*There's never been a better time to be a black American than
during the Trump administration.* Why? Because conservative
policies have led to:

- Record low unemployment
- Record high wage growth
- Booming black business growth

We all recognize the tragic history of ethnic conflict in the
United States, but that's not the country's whole story, obviously. This is the nation that inspired slave revolts around the
world when its own revolution succeeded. This is the nation
that took in more immigrants than any in history and made
them rich. This is the nation that showed a doubled human
lifespan—and a higher standard of living than had before
been thought possible.

America has made mistakes, but America is not a mistake.

Our goal should be to fulfill its promise of freedom, not
debunk that promise. Yet the current generation—the luck-
iest cohort of human beings who have ever lived—want to
be the ones to give it all up. In three centuries, about three
human lifetimes, this country grew to lead the world into
unprecedented health, freedom, and prosperity, but somehow the fashionable political view of the moment among
many members of my generation is socialism. Socialism?

I can't entirely blame them. They're listening to "experts" like the ones who have advised governments for a hundred years to regulate more, tax more, intervene in the economy at every opportunity—to imitate Continental Europe, even when Europe was at its most economically stagnant. But the experts can be wrong, even when armed with statistics. (Remember how wrong they were about Donald Trump's chances of being elected in 2016.) I fear that without America's influence, the experts who encourage socialism would long since have carried the day throughout the world, and there would be no beacon for the devotees of liberty to point to as a counterexample.

I bear no nation ill will, but we know—and most people in other countries know—that it will not be the United Kingdom or Belgium that will determine the future of the world. It will be the United States. To the extent that Trump is the defender and advocate of the United States, he functions as a vessel for Western civilization, which is humanity's best hope of living better than our distant ancestors.

"Our agenda is pro-worker and pro-family," Trump told that 2019 TPUSA crowd. While the phrasing might sound a little like that of a Progressive Democrat, that is because they have condescended from time to time to use populist instead of elitist rhetoric.

He sounded less like a Progressive when he said that the socialist ideas of Representative Alexandria Ocasio-Cortez, Representative Rashida Tlaib, and their allies in Congress are "not American values." To some on the hair-trigger left, this would likely be taken as further evidence that Trump wants to exclude Hispanics and Muslims or that he dislikes women, seeing them as outsiders to a society that should welcome only white males. But he's not objecting to such fringe political figures' last names or ancestry. He's objecting to their desire to break with the practices and values that create the opportunities immigrants come here for.

The MAGA Doctrine is not the belief that one is compassionate toward some families and hostile toward others. Protecting the little guy means protecting the rights of refugees and immigrants, but not at the expense of other Americans' rights or the values that made America unique. It begins with the belief that we should take pride in America's past achievements and recognize that certain beliefs made those achievements possible. Wanting the best for Americans and wanting the ideas of Ocasio-Cortez and her ilk kept at bay are two sides of the same compassionate attitude. We wouldn't wish socialism on our worst enemies—such as, in the second half of the twentieth century, the Russians. They have moved away from socialism in the past thirty years, and we should be smart enough not to repeat the huge mistake they made before that. (In fact, if the Russians have been moving away from socialism, maybe we could afford to be a bit less paranoid about them. We want everyone to wise up and try freedom, and when they do, we can be friends to them all.)

We didn't land men on the Moon, defeat Nazism, defeat Communism in Europe, and create the first society in history where most workers live in air-conditioned comfort by bashing America. We took a certain healthy pride in our way of doing things—not just an arbitrary pride "because it's us" but a rational recognition that humanity has benefited from some of the things America has gotten right.

Students on campuses all over America are being taught to be ashamed of America, but it makes sense to be proud. If shame makes us carelessly adopt ideas antithetical to American success, our shame will be no virtue.

An optimistic America—not a shamed America, nor a hateful and arrogant America—is one of the greatest blessings the world can know. As Trump put it in that same speech, sticking up for America against its enemies and against radically anti-American political ideas isn't a case of wanting a bully to overcome the weak: "It's right overcoming wrong."

We know how the left sees the president. They snicker at images such as the often-shared photo of Trump literally hugging an American flag onstage. What could such a display be except completely cynical theatrics, in their minds? (Since Progressives are very uptight, some might even add that this is technically a violation of official flag-handling protocol, as if they care.) I think, on the contrary, it's Trump at his most heartfelt and honest. He's smiling in that photo not because he thinks he's doing something ridiculous but because he knows he's doing what comes naturally to patriots everywhere. He's happy in that photo! He's celebrating America for a moment, and as he so often does, implicitly giving the rest of us encouragement to carry on that celebration every day.

His idea of fun is celebrating the American flag. Sounds good to me. If that's his idea of mischief, let him be mischievous. It sure beats burning the flag.

If Trump is smart enough to recognize that the values embodied in that flag explain the incredible wealth and happiness of the United States, I'd say he's no dope or reckless redneck. He looks to me more like a stable genius.

Pride in the United States used to be something that both the Republicans and Democrats had in common.

By today's standards, President John F. Kennedy sounded like a conservative when he said, "We dare not forget that we are the heirs of that first revolution"—and Kennedy even sounded a little like Trump when he said, "The American, by nature, is optimistic. He is experimental, an inventor and a builder who builds best when called upon to build greatly."

When Kennedy repeatedly used the old adage that "a rising tide lifts all boats," he was not calling for a complete repudiation of the prior American fashion of doing business. He was not saying, like Democratic representative Ocasio-Cortez in early 2019, that slight improvements on current American policy would be only "10% better than garbage." He would not likely have laughed, like Representative Ilhan Omar in a 2013 interview, at the fact that people say the name *al-Qaeda* with a tone of menace, whereas "you don't say *America* with this intensity," as if—funny thing—to suggest there is something far more dreadful about al-Qaeda.

On the contrary, Kennedy in his inaugural address reaffirmed to the world the special role of the United States, saying, "Let every nation know, whether it wishes us well or ill, that we shall pay any price, bear any burden, meet any hardship, support any friend, oppose any foe, in order to assure the survival and the success of liberty."

(At the same time, to his credit, Kennedy was not an enthusiast of all military intervention, once remarking, according to a source in his administration quoted by the *New York Times*, that he "wanted to splinter the CIA in a thousand pieces and scatter it to the winds" because of its foreign meddling. There are echoes of that sentiment in Trump's wrangles with the Deep State, as he calls it, about which more later.)

Part of what makes the United States great is its capacity to examine and correct its mistakes, to grow. In fact, the right to free speech—and the robust debate it allows about how best to improve this country—is one of America's greatest institutions. But in the six decades since Kennedy's time, a radical, partly post-colonial strain of leftist criticism has arisen that at times treats the United States as we have known it more like a foe than like a beloved parent in need of healing. That specific strain of thought, more subversive than constructive, does have its ultimate roots outside the United States, and it is antithetical to our own philosophical roots.

One of those revolutions I mentioned earlier that took some of its inspiration from ours was the French Revolution of 1789, and at the time the revolutionaries of those two nations and others saw themselves as natural allies, but with the benefit of historical hindsight, America's 1776 and France's 1789 look in some ways like opposites. America's revolution was not so much a break with all prior history as an affirmation of the best lessons learned from that history—and explicitly from British history, even as our country declared its independence from Britain. The English legal tradition was rooted in the rights of the individual and limits on the power of the state and sovereign.

France, at first glance, appeared at once more optimistic and far more pessimistic. The French revolutionaries could not just announce to the world, as America effectively did, that it was a commercial republic separated by an ocean from its former monarch. Monarchy and aristocracy were deeply rooted in every aspect of French society and would not easily be removed. The French revolutionaries, who should perhaps have compromised and remained, as France had briefly been, a constitutional monarchy, decided to tear out the old regime root and branch.

Monarchs, aristocrats, their sympathizers, anyone suspected of sympathizing with them, and, in time, any among the revolutionaries who too loudly questioned the direction of the revolution, could be sentenced to death by guillotine. That viciousness—the sense of a revolution as a sort of purifying fire—is a zeal rarely seen in US history or British history, unless one counts the current fervor of the left's so-called social justice warriors, who do sometimes beat, egg, or Molotov-cocktail their political enemies, though for now they more often just strive to purge their enemies from social media platforms and campus speaking engagements.

The difference between the American Revolution and the French Revolution is the respect for individual liberty.

About forty thousand people were murdered in the French Revolution, sometimes called the Terror. Naturally, the left claims they don't want to repeat the bad parts of revolutionary history—they never do—but the French Revolution was a model for later violent revolutions. While the relatively sedate revolutions going on in the United States and, a century earlier, England itself took their inspiration from individualist philosophers such as John Locke (and coincided with the rise of free-market economics as espoused by thinkers such as Scotland's Adam Smith), the more sweeping and bloody

French Revolution took some of its inspiration from a different strain of the Enlightenment intellectual era: the thought of Jean-Jacques Rousseau.

Rousseau, sounding like a clear forebear of today's leftists, earnestly longed to correct all of society's inequities, beginning almost literally at birth, replacing the immobilizing swaddling clothes and rote educations inflicted (as Rousseau saw it) on helpless children with nature-worshipping, free-spirit-encouraging educations that sound quite pleasant until you hear Rousseau's stealthy hope for those educations: remolding young minds to make them conform to the "General Will" of society, never questioning it—and coming to regard society as a single, unified organism explicitly resembling a phalanx of ancient Spartan soldiers.

A nightmare by Trump-era conservative standards, Rousseau was a little like the ultimate left-wing professor: teaching you just enough to convince you to submit yourself to domination by a super-state. *Non, s'il vous plait.*

It is no accident, as the Marxists would say, that revolutions taking their cues from Rousseau or economic radical Karl Marx would place such an emphasis on denigrating the past. They intended to build things radically new, quite possibly brutal and imperfect, and it wouldn't do to have people pining for the way things used to be. And, after all, the old way was shot through with injustice.

People had to be persuaded, like citizens of Cambodia in the 1970s when the communist Khmer Rouge regime killed nearly a third of the population, that almost everything about the old way of life was evil and had to be eradicated.

In short, people had to feel shame about every aspect of their lives before the new, revolutionary regime, like cult leaders, could be entrusted with total power to make things anew.

That bloody-minded fanaticism had never quite come to the United States, but I fear the constant guilt-trips of today's left, and the constant harping by college professors on all the reasons that mainstream American society should *feel guilty*, are ways of affecting a soft version of those total revolutions from·history—of weakening our resolve to oppose today's anti-American revolutionaries. Constant charges of racism, for example, not just against the president but against almost anyone who dares to honor a literary or philosophical great from the Western canon, or to take inspiration from the music or art of a foreign land without getting the left's permission, or to make an un-PC joke online somewhere, leave malleable young people, in particular, frightened that they will cause outrage if left to make their own decisions.

Free speech is deeply American, and these debates are well worth having—as long as the left doesn't use the institutions they control to punish anyone who debates them.

The temptation grows to let the new revolutionaries call the shots. It's less of a struggle, even if giving up that struggle means part of the American spirit dies.

By contrast, even President Trump's old foe Hillary Clinton would sound a note of traditional American optimism (albeit yoked to Progressive plans) when she said things in her speeches such as "America's best days are still ahead." Would it be heresy for me to say that sounds a little like the futurist sentiment Trump sounds when he says we'll "Make America Great Again"?

The new guilt-trippers don't want to add a few flourishes

to the vibrant America mosaic. They think that Americans, especially those from marginal populations, got shafted by the whole project that is America. This nation is like one ongoing crime in their minds, and it has to be stopped, the perpetrators punished, and a strict rehabilitative regimen imposed (by them).

It sounds cornball, but I'm not ashamed to be an American. I'm not ashamed of America. And I can tell President Trump feels much the same way. Whatever else the MAGA Doctrine may be, it is surely a prescription for making America more fully itself, more recognizable to those who are already this nation's friends, not some invention of the latter-day Rousseaus and Marxes.

CHAPTER 9

An American Great

Like many of his political peers, Donald Trump is rich, estimated to be worth about $3 billion, according to *Forbes* magazine.

It is hinted in his opponents' rhetoric from time to time that there is something scandalous or hypocritical about this, since he talks like a man of the people, eats food from McDonald's, and so forth. But he has made no secret of graduating from the prestigious Wharton business school or making his fortune by going into the real estate business that his father, Fred Trump, went in before him.

One does not as often hear, say, former senator and secretary of state John Kerry's credentials as a spokesman for the American people questioned because of his wife, Teresa Heinz Kerry's, fortune, estimated by *Forbes* at $1 billion. Former senator and vice president Joe Biden talks about his middle-class origins—his dad having gone from oil-family wealth early in life to struggling as a used car sales-man during Joe's childhood—but talks less often about the over $15 million he's made in just the short time since the Obama administration ended, according to his tax returns.

Maybe it's a good sign—a sign of rapidly growing wealth in the United States—that instead of the left being made up of poor people condemning millionaires, it's now made up of millionaires and billionaires condemning multi-billionaires. (Even socialist senator Bernie Sanders famously dropped the "millionaires" part from his angry mentions of "millionaires and billionaires" around the time he became a millionaire himself.)

I hope none of them forget their roots.

Trump's real financial crime, as it were, in the eyes of his peers may be that he sounds to their ears nouveau-riche. As he said to a huge crowd in Fargo, "We got more money, we got more brains, we got better houses and apartments, we got nicer boats, we're smarter than they are, and they say they're the elite."

The president added, "You're the elite; we're the elite."

He's rich, but he's not interested in pretending to be an aristocrat. Instead, he looks like a man who's doing something very American: He's having fun.

It may be his greatest strength. If you look at every presidential contest since the rise of television, it's easy to argue the nomination and the presidency went, every time, to the candidate who looks like they had the most fun.

We can debate his political philosophy and secret, inner-most psychological motivations endlessly, but let's take a moment to marvel at the things about Trump that are most visible and understand why people like them.

Trump has been a larger-than-life personality for decades. He took the time to have funny on-air conversations with radio shock jock Howard Stern. He not only ran beauty pageants but has a stunning ex-model wife. Here is a man who could remain the aloof, cold CEO if he so chose and yet has been willing to throw down in the professional wrestling ring in his numerous WWE appearances, pretending to throw punches and forcibly shave wrestling mogul Vince McMahon. (Is anyone surprised Trump has theatrical tendencies? For many on the left, his association with WWE may be the thing they hate the most.) He is entertaining and likes to have a good time. He takes palpable delight in things like having a helicopter instead of treating such things as just a business necessity.

How can you look on and not sympathize? He's doing the things so many Americans dream of doing. Trump is fun.

One of Trump's fellow New York/New Jersey area celebrities, author Fran Lebowitz, famously and rather insightfully said, "He's a poor person's idea of a rich person. They see him, they think, 'If I were rich, I'd have a fabulous tie like that.'" Critics repeated the line as if it were damaging: Trump the rube, Trump the tacky. Who lines his walls with gold, I mean, really? But the critics were inadvertently reinforcing the idea that Trump is not one of them. He's one of the regular people, the masses over whom Trump's elite critics want to rule. Maybe if they were thinking clearly, the critics could have made Trump sound like evidence of capitalism's excess. They could have tried to out-populist Trump.

Instead, they kept sounding more snotty than he ever does. They thought they understood both wealth and politics—the private sector and the public—better than Trump, but their seeming mastery became a twin liability. They alienated the general public they had so long pretended to be shepherding to a Progressive paradise. When Hillary Clinton tried to label a few hateful Trump supporters "deplorables," Trump supporters got the underlying message clearly enough, as did many moderates: She's looking down on us all.

Only a candidate as inept as Hillary Clinton would show up in a coal state like Kentucky and declare that she would put a lot of coal miners out of work. Only an elitist Massachusetts senator like John Kerry would flaunt his windsurfing while speaking fluent French on the shores of ritzy Monaco. Do these politicians want to make us think of Uncle Sam or Marie Antoinette? And for a long time, both parties have displayed their elite status. The Bushes were proud residents of Kennebunkport, students of Yale, members—like many politicians—of elite secret societies. The American middle class, needless to say, has trouble relating to this.

My good friend Donald Trump Jr. often tells a story of how he would spend weekends with his father on construction sites. The elder Trump would inspect every inch, nook, and cranny. He would even pick up dropped nails from construction sites. Everything counted toward the bottom line. So while the Romneys showed off their dancing horses (not a joke, look it up), George H. W. Bush sped around in a boat in Maine, or John McCain lost track of how many homes he owned while running for president, it was the billionaire from New York who picked up dropped nails and ate McDonald's who related more than anyone to everyday Americans.

That is why he's in the White House and most of the elitist snobs are not.

Some in the media and online have pushed a false narrative that my father, Robert Kirk, designed Trump Tower in New York City. That is untrue, and I've never said it. True, in the 1980s, my father was an entry-level architect, and his firm was involved with the construction of various properties, including Trump Tower. My father interacted with Donald Trump on a handful of occasions, and I remember hearing about Trump's attention to detail and him being a visionary. Today, I work with the president directly on multiple projects. Several times a year, Turning Point USA is invited to the White House, and I can attest to his same focus on detail and his visionary thinking. But there is no connection between my relationship to the president and my father's. Architecture is Dad's department, politics mine. Both those fields and others have been shaped by the recurring figure of Donald Trump.

Though Trump had famously voiced opinions on politics since the 1980s, in interviews with Oprah Winfrey and others, you sensed that he was quite pleased being above the fray. He said time and again that he might run for president if it appeared the country needed him and if he was sure he could win, conditions he didn't think were quite met until the 2016 campaign.

"If I did decide to do it," he told Winfrey in 1988, "I would say that I would have a hell of a chance of winning."

If his interest in politics were just a big publicity stunt, you'd think his views would shift around randomly over the years, but despite some changes in emphasis, certain recognizable themes keep popping up—including his reluctance to wield political power, an admirable trait. He told Winfrey he was hesitant to run. "I probably wouldn't want to rule it out totally because I really am tired of seeing what's happening with this country, how we're really making other people live like kings, and we're not," he said.

In other words: stop being taken advantage of and put America first.

Does a political message of that magnitude and seriousness jibe with spending the 1980s creating a network of lavish casinos sporting names like the Trump Plaza and the Taj Mahal? It does if you think American success looks like people enjoying themselves. At least part of the American story is that, and much of the world loves us for it. They are less enamored of our war-making and our puritanical tendencies—such as our anti-drug crusade that sends helicopters on crop-destroying missions far beyond our borders.

For most of the past century, the Republicans have been playing the part of hectoring moralists. Trump reversed that, revealing what young conservatives already knew: The future of the Democrat Party is whiners and killjoys. The future of the Republican Party is winners.

Americans themselves dream of "livin' large," blowing off steam, throwing a party, and on rare occasions, striking it rich. This country is its mansions and casinos in addition to its churches, malls, corner offices, and suburban homes. We're eclectic. We're not contradictory or losing our sense of purpose by being all of these things. That's America—and Trump is America. Him becoming president is as natural (and as horrifying to the cultural elite) as Reagan becoming president. Reagan was a cross between the cowboy sensibility of the real West and the glamour of Hollywood, with its re-creation of the Old West. The left hated it, but that veneer was accompanied by real, solid conservative principles.

It makes just as much sense for Trump's populist brand of conservatism to be yoked to larger-than-life activities such as building, gambling, wrestling, and, yes, self-promotion. Every American is in advertising, in some sense—and that's OK. It may not look like the quiet, self-effacing Christianity of the Pilgrims or the Amish, it's true, but it's not so out of step with the optimistic, success-oriented message of Trump's childhood pastor, Norman Vincent Peale, the author of *The Power of Positive Thinking*. One book likely influenced by that tract, though it rarely gets touted as a religious tract, is Trump's *Trump: The Art of the Deal*. (Maybe one day it will. Trump himself joked that it was his second-favorite book after the Bible. His coauthor, by contrast, now disavows the book. Trump is a controversial figure, needless to say.)

The shallow way to look at the deal-making side of Trump would be to dismiss him as greedy—believing the worst interpretations of his charitable giving as well—and to see him as a vivid example of America's worst excesses. That attitude is easy to adopt if you view all economics from the

Marxian perspective in which one person's financial gain must be someone else's loss. If that were how economics worked, then indeed a great many people must have lost from Trump's financial activities. But the Marxian seesaw description of economics was never accurate.

To the extent that trade is voluntary—you want something, and I am willing to sell it to you—it's always a plus, or as economists such as Friedman and Mises would say, a mutually beneficial exchange. Not all trades go perfectly or as planned, and many are muted in their benefits by the involvement of nonvoluntary, governmental factors (subsidies, burdensome regulations, etc.), but to the extent everyone involved knew what they were getting into and traded to become a little better off without harming unwitting third parties, the world became a bit better off. In that sense, every deal is a good deal.

And despite decades of left-wing economic propaganda, most Americans, in both parties, seem to understand that. Yahoo Finance reports a survey showing 59% of the public supports the administration's pro-business agenda, and 54% say the businesses with which they work have benefited. America's not turning communist just yet.

Of course, people of my generation, younger millennials, are sometimes put off by any hint of "social conservatism"— religiosity, culture war, what they perceive as excess machismo. And the left tries to paint Trump as a blinkered right-wing culture warrior as surely as they try to paint him as a heartless Dickensian capitalist. But how convincing is the charge, really, aside from what are deliberately provocative tweets and wisecracks?

The man is a New Yorker, after all.

Back in 2000, at the very time Trump was briefly trying to look respectable enough to be worthy of a possible Reform Party presidential nomination, he famously participated in a videotaped sketch for an annual New York media event known as the Inner Circle Show in which he groped then-mayor Rudy Giuliani, who appeared in drag. I'm not saying this is in itself qualification for higher office—and I understand there will be some hard-core social conservatives out there who find such behavior offensive even if obviously done in jest—but I think it's another indicator we're dealing with a man who knows how to laugh at himself and laugh at others without hating them. He's still got Giuliani on his team two decades later.

Whatever else his years in showbiz, casinos, and the rough-and-tumble of New York business did, they didn't produce a humorless, tyrannical ogre, however much it might help the leftists' cause if they had. Most of America keeps laughing with Trump and at the left, even with most of the media trying desperately to make it the other way around.

Who would have imagined, a generation ago when the left's main target on the right was the religiosity of groups such as the Moral Majority, that the day would come when young people, in particular, would think of the Republican president as the one who's in on the joke, the one who understands Twitter and memes, the one who knows how to loosen up a little instead of sounding as if doomsday is right around the corner?

Bizarrely, both Joe Biden and Bernie Sanders may be faring well in the Democratic primary polls for 2020 in part because they resemble Trump a little, not because they oppose him (though they do). With Biden's goofy gaffes and Bernie's rabble-rousing yells, at least the two of them sound a little like they're enjoying themselves. You look at the rest of the Democratic lineup, and you worry that they could almost take lessons from Hillary Clinton on how to have fun, and that's a scary thought.

At the same time, Trump has a sense of duty to something larger than himself. He takes the important things seriously. If he were enamored of power or attention for its own sake, rather than justice, wouldn't he delight in declaring more wars?

If Trump loved authority for its own sake, wouldn't he turn a blind eye to foreign regimes' abuse of their people instead of pushing for the legalization of homosexuality in several truly authoritarian nations? That's a push for which he and his ambassadors get no credit from the left, of course, just as the left rarely notes that Trump was the first president to enter office already endorsing gay marriage, a position the Clintons and Obama only gradually adopted, when it was politically advantageous to do so.

Outside of politics and away from the levers of governmental power, people can continue to call for saintly restraint and decorum, of course.

Overall, Trump looks more like a part of his age cohort—an early baby boomer—than some of his boomer and boomer-influenced critics are probably comfortable admitting. If he has regrets about his own colorful life, then, fittingly, they are likely to be part of a big tapestry, like Sinatra's, that overall contains enough amazing victories to justify the missteps.

And what key attitudes shine through?
He's anti-establishment, you say?
He's anti-war?
He's got an irreverent sense of humor?
He loves liberty, man?
He's letting it all hang out?

Sounds like a boomer after all. I will not insult a great president by suggesting he sounds like a wild hippie, since that's obviously not quite right in describing a suit-wearing, drug-avoiding businessman who went into his dad's business and involves his kids in his own activities. But he sounds more like a man who's coming to set us free than a man who wants to lock us all up.

CHAPTER 10

The Justice Reformer

One of the most important laws in the history of criminal justice reform has been achieved on Trump's watch. It was surprising to people who don't understand the MAGA Doctrine and its focus on helping powerless people who are up against the powerful.

Even the *New York Times* and CNN had to give some credit where it was due on that one, and a big portion of the credit goes to Trump advisor and son-in-law Jared Kushner.

As CNN reported, "The bill's passage is also a win for Kushner, whom the bill's supporters credit with working behind the scenes to steer the legislation past significant opposition within the Trump administration and past shifting coalitions on Capitol Hill."

There had long been recognition on both sides of the political aisle that the war against drugs, whether a good idea or a bad one, doesn't seem to be working. Furthermore, haphazard attempts to create rational, predictable penalties for drug-related crimes had merely produced inflexible "mandatory minimum" sentences that were often denounced for their severity by judges from the bench even as those judges were imposing the sentences.

Compounding those problems, the ostensibly rational sentencing schedules were sometimes in practice quite arbitrary—months for powdered cocaine and years for rock-like "crack," to take the most notorious example.

During the Obama administration, some twenty or so would-be reformers within government met in hopes of coming up with a criminal justice reform plan, from leftists skeptical of law enforcement to right-wingers including Ted Cruz skeptical of government in general. Obama hoped for an omnibus reform bill that would fix all of America's big criminal justice problems simultaneously, combining the best plans from everyone involved, though legislators cautioned him that a plan that ambitious was unlikely to advance in Congress. And most of it didn't.

It's an immense historic irony that a populist president often accused of being an authoritarian—overly sympathetic to police officers—managed, by contrast, to push through a big criminal justice reform bill, complete with the endorsement of a couple of celebrities such as Kim Kardashian, in part by being more pragmatic, more realistic about the issue than his predecessors.

The First Step Act, as it's rightly called—since it is just the beginning of some of those reforms that everyone from Obama to Cruz wanted—was passed because of President Trump and advisors such as Kushner focusing on exactly the sort of marginal citizens the Trump movement is falsely accused of ignoring. The First Step Act gives nonviolent offenders increased ability to earn days off their sentences through good behavior, increasing the odds that they will be more easily acclimated to civilized behavior when back in the outside world (the full name of the bill, Congress craving acronyms, is the Formerly Incarcerated Reenter Society Transformed Safely Transitioning Every Person Act).

You have probably heard a great deal about the conditions in illegal immigrant detention centers (barely any different from the conditions there under Obama), but you probably haven't heard a word from the mainstream media about Trump pushing this law that guarantees female prisoners feminine hygiene products, limits the use of physical restraints on pregnant prisoners, makes the reduction in the crack/powder sentencing disparity retroactive, and mandates training in conflict de-escalation for guards. Signed into law in December 2018, First Step also gives more compassionate leave time to terminally ill prisoners and urges the geographic placement of prisoners close to family, again increasing the odds that they will be acclimated to a normal support network when reintegrated into society.

There is an impulse, often found among traditional conservatives, to think any step in the direction of kindness or leniency toward prisoners is a mistake—softness masquerading as mercy. But assuming prisoners are not simply being executed or put away for life (and there are very, very few prisoners for whom that is the case), it is only rational to be concerned about what their lives, and their states of mind, will be when they have done their time and exited the prison system. It doesn't do innocent, law-abiding citizens any good if prisons are merely a system for turning criminals into even more violent, even angrier, even more dysfunctional members of society. Easing them back in helps everyone.

Consider what an embarrassment the First Step Act should be for the liberal establishment.

Democratic presidential candidates for 2020 want you to take it for granted they're the compassionate ones, Trump the heartless "law-and-order" candidate from a party that uses the drug war as an excuse to harass minorities. But look at the track records of Senators Joe Biden and Kamala Harris. Biden pushed for harsher sentences in the late 1980s and criticized then–president George H. W. Bush for not going far enough, saying Bush's plan "doesn't include enough police officers to catch the violent thugs, not enough prosecutors to convict them, not enough judges to sentence them, and not enough prison cells to put them away for a long time."

Biden would spend much of the 1990s making up for what he saw as the drug war's softness by using his position as head of the Senate Judiciary Committee to push longer sentences and the creation of more prisons. It is in no small part thanks to Joe Biden that the United States has the highest incarceration rate in the world, with about two million of the Earth's total prison population of around nine million located here. About 0.7% of the US population is in prison.

That's about twice the rate of imprisonment in Russia and five times the rate in China, which together with the United States account for about half the world's prison population, one American statistic that shouldn't evoke pride, whether you think our problem is too many arrests or too many badly behaved people, or both.

As catalogued by an April 25, 2019, Vox.com article,

Biden's record includes shepherding 1980s and '90s laws that expanded the use of civil asset forfeiture (seizing the property of people caught with even small amounts of drugs on the assumption whatever they own might be the fruits of drug profits), increased the powder/crack disparity (increasing the racial disparity in sentencing as a side effect), and increased prison funding in order to allow for an expanded prison population. Biden has sent mixed messages since, apologizing for some effects of the laws, promoting counseling for ex-prisoners, and beginning in 2010 to work with then–President Obama to reduce the powder/crack disparity Biden had helped create.

But he still touted his tough-on-crime record on the campaign trail. Vox quotes *Washington Post* columnist Radley Balko's conclusion that "The martial/incarceral state has had no greater friend in Washington over the last 35 years than Joe Biden."

Kamala Harris, by contrast, has brought about fewer changes in her role in the Senate. Her opposition to unreasonable bail requirements is an admirable exception—and, to her credit, she has argued in favor of laws allowing prisoners to get high school diplomas—but she was an extremely aggressive drug warrior and prosecutor during her time before that as California's state attorney general, even allowing the state attorneys working under her to fight to keep people in prison after they were proven innocent, if they had missed filing deadlines for relevant legal forms. She also defended law enforcement officials who got convictions by withholding evidence or falsifying confessions. It is terrifying to think that about an eighth of the US prison population lives in a state with such a coldly bureaucratic conception of justice.

(She may have had coldly careerist notions about sex back in the '90s as well, since she notoriously slept with San Francisco assembly speaker Willie Brown, who was still married at the time, as he appointed her to a series of well-paid city positions.)

It is hard to imagine someone like Harris becoming a merciful president, if American citizens find themselves running afoul of overly harsh regulations. As for Biden, he'll shift with the political winds as he always has, talking like a champion of desegregation today but opposing busing of students to integrate racially homogeneous school districts four decades ago. Harris flip-flops as well, sometimes making it difficult to determine what her position is on a given law. She at times opposed California's three-strikes-you're-out (for life) laws—but then again, she wanted to jail parents if their kids skipped school.

She's not shy about coming down on people with the hammer of government. Is there any person who better represents the opposite of what the MAGA Doctrine dictates?

Four more years of President Trump looks like the humane choice. With a Republican Congress, while he had one, he got more done on criminal justice reform than the Democrats, who claim to be such bleeding hearts. (Trump is capable of working across the aisle, though, and his call for a Second Step Act to continue the cause of criminal justice reform helped inspire Senator Cory Booker's introduction of a bill by that name designed to ease restrictions on employment for ex-convicts. Productive ex-prisoners are less likely to re-offend than ones who are left on the margins of society with no means of support.) Best of all, Trump appears to understand the distinction between violent and nonviolent offenders, which is more than can be said for most politicians. Great countries don't usually incarcerate people who haven't hurt anyone.

As a New Yorker, Trump may well have learned from the unfortunate experience of the Rockefeller Drug Laws, which replaced the experience and judgment of judges with a table of mandatory sentences, creating a model soon used throughout the country, ostensibly for making the drug war more rational and predictable. Instead, even in the face of changing scientific evidence about drugs and the potential for treatment over imprisonment, mandatory minimum rules enshrined harsh penalties as if in stone.

We've reached the point at which the drug war itself has done about as much damage as drugs. President Trump reminds us it is still possible to temper justice with mercy, to the benefit of everyone involved. A president who gets called racist by the media nearly every day has worked hard to undo some of the overexpansion of the prison population—which happened in part under President Bill Clinton in the '90s as he strove to prove that liberals can be as "serious" about crime-fighting as law-and-order conservatives. Yet Bill Clinton got rewarded with the affectionate joke—started by Toni Morrison—that he was in some ways America's "first black president" because of his humble beginnings, love of fast food, and betrayal by the donor class.

If Trump increased the number of young, black males behind bars as much as Clinton, Biden, and Harris have, they'd say it was evidence he's Hitler reincarnated.

Just as it would be simplistic to treat Trump's views on military action as merely "anti-war" or "pro-war," since he is trying to be selective and smart about the use of the military, it is wrong to treat his attitude toward crime (or any politician's attitude toward crime, really) as one of "toughness" or "leniency." The question is which crimes, which responses.

Trump sounds tough to the point of ruthlessness in his critics' minds, but he wants results. You see it not only in his periodically updated agenda but in the appointments he makes. If former attorney general Jeff Sessions had developed a foolproof plan to achieve the sweeping victories in the drug war that eluded all of his predecessors, Trump might well be in favor of it.

The American public tends to think the same way. They aren't hard-core ideologues, but they want politicians to keep their word, and they want policies that yield the results advertised. Those aren't unreasonable demands. But they're demands that are rarely met in politics. In politics, unlike the world of business, not accomplishing anything can be its own kind of success. The only "results" most politicians are interested in are the votes in the next election.

Trump wants to solve problems. His emphasis on tackling the opioid crisis is evidence he's not just indifferent to all recreational drug use. But he knows when to abandon a losing tactic, unlike most people in Washington who are content to keep trying the same strategies over and over again for decades (literally, in the case of the war on drugs, which has been going on for about fifty years now).

He hasn't quite yet decided to abandon the whole drug war—though at times he has expressed sympathy for letting the fifty states experiment with different approaches, one way to discover if there's a policy out there that works better than what we've been doing. He knows, though, that locking up 0.7% of the population hasn't done the trick, and more of the same probably won't enable us to turn some magical corner in the drug war.

Trump's brother Fred died from alcoholism at age forty-three, likely influencing Trump's own decreased consumption of alcohol over the years. Trump probably doesn't think that raiding his brother's home with a SWAT team at 3 a.m. and threatening to put him in prison would have been the most humane solution to his addiction. A great country doesn't give up on its addiction-plagued citizens, and it doesn't just shoot them or lock them up and throw away the key. It has the patience to keep searching for solutions, and that will probably involve changes in law, culture, and our understanding of psychology. As with broader criminal justice reform, it will be a long-term, evolving process.

So, too, the reform of the healthcare system, which, as we'll see, has a lot more problems than just excess opioid distribution.

CHAPTER 11

Making America
Well Again

The Republican Party repeatedly promised to repeal Obamacare—but there were grim pronouncements that the law was just too complex to get rid of cost-effectively. It was already shaping the behavior of too many doctors, hospitals, and insurance companies to uproot.

A Republican-appointed Supreme Court chief justice, John Roberts, gave Obamacare the final blessing by voting not to overturn it, reasoning that the "individual mandate" at the heart of the Affordable Care Act wasn't an authoritarian penalty, designed to make people engage in commerce they didn't want to engage in. According to Roberts, the mandate was just a tax after all, and thus within Congress's power to levy, even though the whole Obamacare package, the Affordable Care Act, had been shoved through Congress in part through the rationale that the individual mandate wasn't a tax—and thus that finalizing the whole bill during a "reconciliation process" (the Senate and the House supposedly working out mere clashing details) was legally acceptable, no big deal.

Obamacare wasn't a tax when it needed to avoid being a tax, then it was a tax when it needed to be one to survive a constitutional challenge. Voila, socialized medicine in America takes another stealthy leap forward.

But then Trump managed to undo that sometimes-a-tax-sometimes-not-a-tax, in an underappreciated detail of his 2017 tax reform bill. The bill didn't formally repeal Obamacare. It just lowered the penalty for failing to buy mandated health insurance to $0. I can think of a lot more laws that would benefit from a penalty that size.

The individual mandate summed up so much that is wrong with the way twenty-first-century liberals think about their role in society. Faced with the undeniable fact that some people have difficulty paying for healthcare— thanks in large part to regulations and tax rules decades ago that herded most employees into a tiny handful of corporate health insurance packages provided through their employers, erasing real competition and the price transparency found in most normal purchases—Obama-era liberals decided to "help" the uninsured by just ordering them to buy health insurance.

Not so great for people who calculated that they could get by without it for a short time to pay other bills—but great for the insurance companies, who suddenly had a whole new swath of involuntary customers. It's a little like the logic behind minimum wage laws: Liberals wish you had a higher-paying job, so they're going to outlaw the lower-paying one in which you currently work. Gee, thanks.

Trump's approach to healthcare may be the best example of the new conservative approach. In the past, the parties have had to decide whether to side with big businesses, the insurance companies, the hospitals, or the American Medical Association if they wanted to get anything done. Instead, Trump has repeatedly sided with individuals and small businesses.

One of the big criticisms of Trump's elimination of the individual mandate is that if millions of young people seize the opportunity to stop paying for health insurance, Obamacare-linked health insurance programs will go bankrupt. They'll be paying out to the old and the infirm without being subsidized by the steady flow of young, healthy (involuntary) customers they'd been counting on. Now, warn critics, the whole system may implode because of the financial imbalance.

But is this the fault of Trump? Is this the fault of the young people being dragooned into participating in the system?

It's bad enough that we pay for things through insurance in the first place. No one can keep track of who owes what to whom: patients, doctors, insurance companies, pharmacies, and on and on. So much easier if you knew the price up front and knew when it was fully paid. But insurance companies, if they're going to be involved in something as complex as healthcare at all, are surely responsible for doing their math homework to see whether their businesses are profitable. It shouldn't be one giant pyramid scheme in which the young keep having to be suckered in—or thanks to Obamacare while the mandate existed, forced in—to keep the payments going out on the other end to the more infirm.

There's no reason an activity that could be run like any other free-market business—with competition to provide better service and lower prices—should be forced to operate like this. Even if we conclude that the government must subsidize poorer customers, let everyone make their healthcare purchases as individuals on the open market as they please. Then we can help pick up the tab for the very poorest among us, whether through charity or, if absolutely necessary, government.

Our employers have more important things to do than shop for our insurance plans on our behalf, and continuing to rely on employer-provided healthcare is what makes our current system so uneven and opaque. Please leave my generation out of it, or at least let us start opting out if we think we can get a better deal. Or even take our chances without health insurance, while the current crazy system lasts.

Whether giving employers tax breaks that they can only get by opting into a few big, government-approved health insurance plans, or forcing the young to get health insurance, it sure seems as if there's a pattern, one that has existed for decades, of "progressive" reform plans always ending up giving a big boost to one industry or another, without necessarily rescuing the poor. Free-marketeers pointed out a similar problem on President George W. Bush's watch when he pushed through a massive subsidy for pharmaceuticals for the elderly as part of Medicare.

It sounds nice, but a subsidy for the drug purchases of the

elderly is also, of course, a great big subsidy for the pharmaceutical industry. They were no doubt as worried about the older adults not buying drugs as the insurance industry was about young people not buying insurance. The answer is not to have government do the buying for industry. The answer might be for industry to compete to offer much better deals, not get locked in a big-government plan that may stagnate and not see any further innovations for decades to come.

The thicket of regulations that has grown up around healthcare and health insurance—partly because employers wanted goodies to offer employees at a time when they were forbidden to raise wages by Nixon's onerous wage and price controls—will have to be unwound with care.

Trump's proposed American Patients First reform plan should be a big step in the right direction.

I would not, in any case, assume the Democrats know what a healthy America looks like when they see it. San Francisco, Nancy Pelosi's district, has more drug addicts than students enrolled in public high school. Democrats destroy everything they touch, but they'll always insist they did so for compassionate reasons and that the Republicans are cruel by contrast.

One key element of Trump's American Patients First plan, at least in its inchoate form in late 2019, is simply mandating that customers see the prices for medical services clearly and transparently posted before they agree to treatments.

In any other business, this idea wouldn't be regarded as the least bit strange. It's not radical. It's just common sense.

Yet look at the nonsense words—disguised as free-market, consumer-friendly rhetoric—spouted by big businesses deeply enmeshed in the current healthcare regime:

"Publicly posting privately negotiated rates could, in fact, undermine the competitive forces of private market dynamics and result in increased prices," said Rick Pollack, CEO of the American Hospital Association, according to a June 25, 2019, article on ModernHealthcare.com. The group America's Health Insurance Plans held a similar position.

And according to the article, Justine Handelman, a senior vice president at the Blue Cross and Blue Shield Association, said, "We need to ensure consumers have information that is relevant to their decision-making, while ensuring disclosure of information does not raise costs or jeopardize the privacy and security of consumers' personal health information."

If this were a simple transaction between you—the patient/buyer—and your doctor in a competitive market, this sudden concern for privacy might be understandable, but these are conglomerates produced precisely by the perverse public/private partnership created between government regulators, including tax collectors, and a handful of the biggest insurance companies. The idea that they don't want you knowing how they calculate prices because you might become confused or because it might make the whole medical industry more prone to careless personal-data-sharing than it is already is just ludicrous.

What the calcified health insurance companies are afraid of is that if you see how wildly and arbitrarily prices vary—and how much you're being charged for real medical services vs. bureaucratic mark-ups—you and hundreds of millions of other Americans will wake up and start demanding real choice and flexibility, not just Options A, B, and C from your employer's plan for your entire physical well-being (and likely that of your family).

President Trump had his differences with the late Senator John McCain, but one of several things McCain got right during his failed 2008 campaign for the presidency was making the separation of employer and healthcare central to his healthcare reform proposal. While candidate Obama was dreaming of expanding government involvement in health and lying about whether his reform plan would enable you to "keep your doctor," McCain wanted to sever the healthcare plan connection to your boss so that you'd be more likely to get the plan you want, providers would face new competitive pressure to keep more-mobile customers, and workers would be a little more courageous about switching jobs to boot.

Make people less nervous about their health coverage, and they'll behave a little more confidently in general. Transparency and transportability in health insurance is a good start. The alternative is an exercise in blind trust—hoping your boss and your doctor and your insurance company all know what they're doing and care, really care, about you. Blind trust tends to erode after a while. Then people get suspicious.

And from time to time, a suspicious populace engages in populist rebellion. Maybe healthcare is overdue for one.

While the common citizen may be no expert, and may be wrong in some cases, the common citizens' distrust of the establishment has been well-earned. That distrust is never stoked more intensely than when big government and big business collude. Those two forces are dangerous enough separately—and each pretends to be at war with the other, at least for about a hundred years now, ever since Teddy Roosevelt and Woodrow Wilson made it popular to denounce the power of corporations in a democracy. But what goes on behind closed doors when government and business join forces? Do they expect us to believe each side—either side—is fiercely fighting for our interests instead of its own?

I do not mean to suggest that doctors want to neglect their patients or milk them for the most money possible. However, even doctors admit they have difficulty keeping track of which procedures are covered by which reimbursement amounts in both government-run plans such as Medicare and the insurance-company-run health plans the tax code steers employers into.

Even if only on a subconscious level, this is an incentive for people who stand to benefit from the money sloshing around in the bureaucracy to steer coverage in the direction of their companies, their areas of medical expertise, or their insurance compensation rules.

You probably know people who dutifully paid their health insurance premiums for years only to discover that, by some unforeseen technicality, they aren't covered when a devastating health problem hits. The health insurance companies are rarely outright lying about the coverage—and your doctor may find the situation as infuriating as you do—but this is the deadening (and sometimes deadly) bureaucracy that arises when doctors, patients, insurers, and employers all get used to assuming that someone else is ultimately responsible for making the important decisions, for economizing and seeking efficiency, in healthcare.

The long-term solutions to this problem will require overhauling about a seventh of the US economy—even as the average age of Americans increases and more of us require medical services as a result. But we should at least begin by throwing the harsh light of economic clarity across the health bureaucracy. Prices are signals, as the Austrian School economists teach us. They show us where to devote resources and what's not worth it.

Let us see those prices. Let us see the lazy, bureaucratic backdoor dealing going on between medical services, insurers, and government that ends up producing our incomprehensible and large bills. Making America's healthcare system great again will first require knowing when we're getting a great deal versus when the system is just adding insult to our injuries.

CHAPTER 12

The Tech Sector

Trump has been called a conservative or nationalist—and called much worse things by his enemies—but also a populist, someone who rightly or wrongly presents himself as a sort of tribune of the people, offering to defend them against the elite. The last time America saw a boom in self-consciously populist politics, the late nineteenth century, that mood went hand in hand with "trust-busting," that is, the search for checks on the growing power of corporations over American life.

Today, we'd refer to similar efforts as "breaking up monopolies," and it's a controversial idea in conservative circles because it means government interference with free markets. When you look closely at a monopoly, you can almost always find a government-enforced barrier to entry. Instead of breaking up a major player, politicians are better off looking for ways to encourage more companies to compete with that major player. It's never smart to fight overregulation with more regulation.

Indeed, there was fear in the late nineteenth century that the trust-busting mood would lead to socialism. In the early twentieth century, both Republican president Teddy Roosevelt and Democratic president Woodrow Wilson took pains to say that as Progressives, they were offering a middle-of-the-road alternative to socialism. In the century since, the US government has become less of a hammer smashing monopolies and more of a deeply entwined vine, its regulations mixing at every point with corporate practices. The trusts were tamed instead of busted.

Faced with the clash between corporations and socialism, then, the early twentieth-century Progressives instead opted to add just a little of the latter to the former. As a result, free-market advocates, including most conservatives, were delighted in the 1990s when the emerging Internet was treated as something government should largely butt out of. Even today, when virtually every nook and cranny of American life is taxed, it's controversial to suggest taxing various online activities, even ordinary shopping. That's a victory for the market and a welcome limitation on government.

So, too, is the recognition that computer technology advances so quickly that bumbling federal regulators would probably do nothing but damage if they waded into the industry and started telling innovators what to do. They'd be recommending 1960s IBM solutions to a world changing so quickly Linux will probably be obsolete one day soon. And they'd be making their recommendations in long, boring hearings at which it would become apparent that some members of Congress weren't sure what the Internet is.

So, what, if anything, is to be done about Google? What, if anything, is to be done about the power of social media companies?

Psychologist Robert Epstein, who describes himself as a past Hillary Clinton supporter and has been an NPR commentator and *Psychology Today* editor-in-chief, warned in a 2019 Senate Judiciary Committee hearing that Google could easily shift several million votes to one candidate or another in a presidential election, through just the tiniest of alterations to its algorithms, suppressing a negative article here, boosting the profile of a positive article there. Google swears it has done no such thing—indeed that it has never "manually" altered the ranking outcomes for search items.

However, that's asking us to put a great deal of trust in an organization whose past CEO, Eric Schmidt (he held various leadership positions with Google and its parent company Alphabet from 2001–2017), was an advisor to the Obama 2008 campaign and who started a company that did consulting work for Hillary Clinton throughout her 2016 campaign. Google sells to both companies and political campaigns its ability to influence the public, and at the same time wants us to believe it does nothing to subtly influence that public at those times when the smallest nudges could yield the biggest changes in the state of the world.

Anecdotal evidence suggests that searches for embarrassing stories on Clinton, for instance, when performed on other search engines yield the sorts of results you'd expect but on Google cough up pages of results debunking the criticisms. It's hard to say. Google's algorithm is proprietary, and search results vary in a personalized way with the user as well.

But what Robert Epstein knows as a psychologist is how much difference little nudges can make, especially when multiplied by hundreds of millions of users. Whether or not it has yet been abused, that is an awesome power to be vested in the hands of one company.

We have a window into how Google thinks when it does take an active hand in shaping content, in the form of the rules for use of YouTube, which Google owns.

The Canadian conservative psychologist Jordan Peterson found himself locked out of his Google and YouTube accounts without explanation after he criticized the transgender movement—not advocating violence or hate, merely reaffirming that he thinks there are two biologically rooted genders. But that, combined with the Canadian government's warnings it would treat anti-trans sentiment as bigotry, was likely enough to get Peterson frozen out for a few days despite his immense popularity (indeed, were he not so popular, popular enough to make a stink and get other well-known pundits tweeting and posting about the ban, it's possible he would have remained permanently locked out by Google/YouTube).

It's hard to say for sure because YouTube gave him no explanation, and the same is true of many other conservative, libertarian, and non-mainstream leftist voices on YouTube. They might not all find themselves banned outright, but YouTube has other ways of punishing dissenters, most notoriously "demonetizing" videos so that ads do not appear on them, meaning the people who posted the videos make no revenue from them—while their approved rivals continue to rake it in.

The power of social media platforms such as Google, You-Tube, and Facebook to determine the bounds of acceptable discourse is unnerving enough when the president and his allies in government are butting heads with the liberals who run those platforms. What would it be like—realistically, we should say what *will* it be like—one day when those platforms are completely allied with the administration in Washington, presumably a left-leaning one, perhaps some-day even a left-leaning one that dominates all three branches at the same time?

President Trump sparring with tech companies may not always be pretty, but it beats watching the tech companies quietly blend into the state. Already, we know that the Deep State, US intelligence agencies that may be more loyal to their own agendas than to a given president, from time to time makes requests of the major social media companies, not to mention Amazon, to hand over user data that might help the government in an investigation (and the companies, to their credit, often resist if they do not think the users' suspected activities rise to the level of terrorism or criminal-ity). What happens if those tech companies one day have as collegial and enthusiastic a relationship with the government as Eric Schmidt did with Obama and Clinton?

There is reason for a bit more paranoia here than is caused by asking what the nationalization of just any industry might look like. Traditional industries are fat, slow-moving targets compared to ephemeral social media. Traditional industries build things, sell them, ship them. We can see the results, tote up the widgets hauled.

If the tech sector in its search engine–controlling and social media–managing form blends with the state, by contrast, we will be in the hands of the most advanced, algorithmic, artificial-intelligence-assisted, stealthy means for influencing public opinion the world has ever known.

And this, too, will harken back to the days of Woodrow Wilson in a way. Madison Avenue public relations firms arose hand in hand with the modern military as Woodrow Wilson pushed the United States into World War I and expanded the domestic role of government as well. There is a longstanding precedent for the heads of media, military, and economic regulation to work in tandem, though they do not call too much attention to their collusion and sometimes make a big show of their internal divisions and clashes.

We could simply hope for the best, assume that despite the incredible power to shape public opinion the tech sector is amassing, it will not abuse that power or collude with some factions in government against others. On one hand, of course, the tech companies, like all of us (even presidents) are presumed innocent until proven guilty. On the other hand, the tech companies have given us so many reasons to worry already. They assure us AI personal assistants Siri and Alexa aren't listening to us and sharing our conversations with human analysts back at their parent companies—until they belatedly admit, oh, yes, they are doing that, though the way we were asked about it by the press or Congress didn't technically match the methods we use and thus didn't mandate full disclosure on our part.

You thought when you got a device that could react to

your voice commands it would be able to search for shopping items you requested. You just weren't savvy enough to realize what that meant was that the personal assistant would be listening to you have sex, or your children talking about their deepest fears, with those sounds archived for later sharing with big teams of human researchers back at the company. Apparently you don't understand contracts—or didn't stop to think what you were signing onto when you clicked a little box saying your data could be used to help determine what ads and services to send you.

Foolish you, thinking there's anything sinister about all this. Meanwhile, reports emerge that the doorbell cameras Amazon provided customers to spot deliveries and visitors are also sharing their footage with police departments. What will it be next?

All of this at least raises questions about how we interpret static, old-fashioned contracts, including implicit ones between customer and service-provider, in an era in which the technology that matters most in your life next year may not even exist when you check that little box on the user form this year.

If populism, then, looks to the pure free-marketeer like a blunt instrument being used to slam both big government and big business, maybe it's not because populism is retrograde and Luddite. Maybe populism is avant-garde. Maybe, like the complaints of conservatives banned from Twitter that they're being excluded from contemporary democratic discourse—which at first sound maudlin and perhaps even like an inappropriate attempt to tell a private media company what to do—populism is a necessary, historically adaptive response to changing technology.

Yes, regulating social media or breaking up Google could have clear downsides. Injecting more government power and politics into Google is likely to lead to an even more powerful and politicized government-Google partnership. However, without greater transparency and assurance of fairness, the social media companies will rightly remain targets of suspicion—especially when they sometimes already collude with government.

Well before critics started complaining that in Trump we have a conspiracy theorist for a president, former CIA and National Security Agency staffer Edward Snowden woke the world up to the domestic snooping potential such agencies have, how massive databanks are already warehousing metadata, at the very least, about all our online communications and phone calls. That was a big enough blow to public trust. What happens when the walls between such agencies and the tech sector erode? And what happens if the government cannot peer into and police social media practices?

You can already see this on the horizon with billion-dollar companies like Palantir. A private company with little transparency, they work extensively with hedge funds, banks, and manufacturers. However, they also work for almost every part of the government, processing data on terrorist suspects, illegal immigrants, and potentially illegal financial transactions.

Populism arises in part from the sneaking suspicion that whatever balance of power is worked out between big-government and big-business forces, the average citizen's say in it all will be quite small. If James Comey and other Obama allies could spy on candidate Trump and lie about it, and the latest documents released suggest that is the case, what hope is there for the privacy of the average citizen? Yet that same spying government is often the only tool big enough to challenge deceptive behavior by companies as powerful as Google and Facebook have become.

If serious rivals to those companies do not arise soon in the marketplace without government getting more deeply involved, I think some sloppy government-mandated solution is almost inevitable, possibly including antitrust legal action against the big tech companies. I would prefer it didn't come to that.

Hong Kong might provide a glimpse of what a future populist revolt against an otherwise untouchable tech regime could look like. If you can't trust online communication (or mainstream media), at some point you take to the streets in protest.

For years, the Chinese government has been developing an elaborate online "social credit system" for tracking citizens and determining what benefits they'll receive for good behavior, which is of course to say obedient behavior that doesn't challenge the government. Beijing has had a little help in shaping its online totalitarian architecture from Google, which has been working on a skewed search system that doesn't return information banned by the Communist Chinese government. It's the kind of results-tweaking Google says it would never do, at least domestically—and yet they're working on similar search censorship for the United States, presumably one that will be fully mandatory, without the force of communist legal compulsion.

And yet I have to wonder how much difference that will

make if the system ends up determining people's credit ratings, access to social media, perhaps even ability to open a bank account. It is troubling that our tech companies would be comfortable working, or at least considering working, with Beijing after all the times those companies have suffered the theft of their intellectual property by China (or at least China's routine failure to enforce intellectual property claims, one of the reasons for Trump's heightened "trade war" and punitive tariff threats against that country).

Then again, it is also amazing that Silicon Valley overwhelmingly donates to Democrats despite all the regulatory and tax roadblocks the Democrats throw in the way of commerce and innovation.

Whether in China or the United States, though, one common way to cope with a regime of constant monitoring is simply to keep your head down. Don't do or say anything risky. Most people in the United States already take that approach on social media—joking about not wanting a rude comment on Twitter to end up being mentioned in a job interview five years later. In Hong Kong, where the risks have been greater since it was formally taken over by the Communist mainland government in 1997, for two decades there have been worries about creeping "self-censorship." The little island city-state with the big economy in theory retained virtually all of its rights from before 1997, the inheritance of a century and a half of British rule.

But if you're a newspaper editor or TV journalist there considering whether to mention some minor story reflecting badly on the new rulers in Beijing, it may just be easier . . . not to.

And yet in mid-2019 we saw people take to the streets of

Hong Kong in protest, despite all the overwhelming force at Beijing's disposal and its thorough lock on people's "social credit" scores, complete with travel bans and hiring restrictions for the disobedient. People can still rebel. And to the horror of some leftist journalists back in the United States, it seems they can even adopt American symbols such as our flag as emblems of freedom. Recall, similarly, that American blue jeans were sometimes a symbol of rebellion in the Soviet Union, jazz enraged the Nazis, dumped tea marked the start of our own revolution against the Brits, and you never quite know what the next free-floating imagery denoting freedom will be.

In fact, it's interesting that the far right and far left are often in agreement on the importance of transparency about the rules of speech at the big tech companies (and in government). After all, it's the people on the fringes who get censored first. The cozy establishment liberals like Hillary Clinton are safe. They're the ones who define what's considered safe discourse, so no centrally mandated "etiquette" rules are ever likely to scare them. I might get censored by some social media platform. A far-left commentator like Tim Pool might get censored. Joe Biden, I promise you, never will be.

So one thing we should be on the lookout for, as we urge greater transparency, not greater censorship, from online media, is the kind of mission creep we see from European Union regulators. To their credit, they see the dangerous potential of social media. To their credit, they call out social media companies for lying about their internal practices (in business, that's called fraud, after all). But government rarely stops at just punishing fraud, which would accomplish so much. Instead, for example, the European Union has begun pressuring Facebook to take down any posts it deems hateful. And then the definition of hate expands to include criticism of mass immigration and open borders. (And for the coup de grâce, American companies adopt whatever practices over here would keep the EU regulators happy over there—and our liberties erode out of a quest for globalized efficiency, as surely as if we were ruled from Brussels instead of Washington.)

You can see the potential for a similar definitional creep in the United States. A left-leaning company that would like to silence conservatism can do it by slowly redefining what is unacceptable online conduct. You start out tracking terrorists. Then you forbid any violent threats, which is reasonable. Then you start claiming that no users should be made to feel "unsafe." Then you start deploying the broad campus-activist definition of unsafe. Then any advocacy of policies that the left thinks might, in the long run and in a roundabout way, make citizens in general less safe, becomes forbidden speech. Heck, let's label it "hate speech" while we're at it.

And somehow, bit by bit, you find yourself trapped in a mental cell in which only talking in ways compatible with leftist policy is deemed safe, nonviolent, non-hateful discourse.

And the more pervasive and powerful social media becomes, the more corners of our life are made tech-compliant and "smart," the more this shrinking of acceptable discourse can happen without ever quite running afoul of the First Amendment, which after all properly limits only government, not private institutions.

This is going to yield a culture war that may be more complex and harder to resolve than the traditional right-vs.-left, religion-vs.-secularism, corporate-vs.-activist divides. The tech companies, in the most dire assessment, may become the most powerful example of capitalism turned against itself. Lenin joked that capitalists are so dumb and greedy we'd sell communists the rope with which to hang us. I hope we don't one day conclude that technology and capitalism made possible the social media culture in which the voices of capitalism and the right get silenced, almost as effectively as in China.

With the mediated, technological component of our lives only likely to get bigger, we might find our culture struggling with how to handle tech and communication long after current wars and border struggles have faded into history. To be sure, the days when nearly all Americans could agree on the same basic rules of etiquette to tamp down such disputes are long gone.

For now, though it may be arbitrary and cagey about its speech rules, at least Twitter is enough of a free-for-all to include President Trump's account, a source of daily joy and frequent hilarity.

The subtler question is how much the social media companies foreground or downplay the frequency with which we see such users as they do allow. It's nice to live in an era wrestling with a question that subtle—beats being told you'll be shot if you insult the Communist Party. If you live in a country where you can openly call the leader a fascist, you don't live in a fascist country! But subtler can also be creepier. Little nudges can make big differences in our lives without inspiring the reflex to fight back. You may never know what online posts, what political ads, what criticisms of immigration, what gun-purchasing advice you never got to see. No one can know how much our individual online experiences have been tailored, much less how much they have been tailored to exclude conservative content.

I realize that to many on the left, the idea that the MAGA Doctrine includes a thoughtful free speech plank would seem shocking. To them, Trump is merely the president who constantly insults the press and thus a threat to the First Amendment itself. That is a misunderstanding of what it means to have a free press. Trump shouldn't censor—and hasn't. His private company can sue, as it sued MSNBC host Lawrence O'Donnell for suggesting that company was funded by Russian oligarchs.

But he has no intention of outlawing even the media he complains about most, and he has said that explicitly, even while ribbing the likes of Rosie O'Donnell. He's just exercising his free speech as she exercises hers, and he plainly loves that sort of low-level ongoing debate and mockery and wouldn't have it any other way.

Far from being the menace to the First Amendment the thin-skinned press makes him out to be, President Trump may be the greatest defender the Bill of Rights has in modern America. Let's count the ways.

CHAPTER 13

Protector of the Bill of Rights

The site Huffington Post warns of "Trump's War on the First Amendment." PEN American Center executive director Suzanne Nossel, formerly executive director of Amnesty International USA, writes that "Trump's Divisive Speech Puts the First Amendment at Risk."

Trump criticizes the media—though he would have to tweet very rapidly indeed to criticize them as often as they criticize him. He has half-jokingly wondered aloud whether some TV news networks deserve to have their broadcast licenses revoked for lying, but that's not even his call. It's the FCC's, and even the FCC doesn't have the power to censor views or close down a whole network. At most, they could yank the broadcast licenses of individual, local stations. The Internet would remain almost unassailable even then.

But this is all hypothetical—and a little ridiculous. Trump is not going to shut down the media. What he is going to do is something that bothers journalists far more than government action. (They seem to like government action most of the time, in fact.) He's going to keep criticizing them. That isn't a threat to the First Amendment. It's part of the endless debate the First Amendment makes possible.

Trump has a good record as a defender of the whole Bill of Rights (to take just the most well-known part of our Constitution, its first ten Amendments). Consider:

The First Amendment

Congress shall make no law respecting an establishment of religion, or prohibiting the free exercise thereof; or abridging the freedom of speech, or of the press; or the right of the people peaceably to assemble, and to petition the Government for a redress of grievances.

In addition to leaving the press unmolested, Trump took an important symbolic action against one stealthy, growing threat to free speech. If the government subsidizes universities, and those universities increasingly restrict what students can say (at an important, politically formative time in their lives and on campuses that are incubators for later political organizing in the adult world), the government is in effect outsourcing censorship to academia.

Officially, Congress's hand stays clean, but indirectly government thereby strikes a terrible blow to our culture, undermining the willingness of young people to engage in open-ended, free-spirited political discussion, especially if they want to speak up in favor of rights like the ones enshrined in the Constitution, as opposed to ones conjured by "social justice" advocates.

President Trump invited members of my group, Turning Point USA, to be present at the White House on March 21, 2019, when he signed an executive order warning colleges that receive federal funding that they have a duty to respect their students' First Amendment rights. The president also mentioned our organization on multiple occasions during the event, complimenting the work we are doing on campuses across the country.

As the president put it, "We reject oppressive speech codes, censorship, political correctness, and every other attempt by the hard left to stop people from challenging ridiculous and dangerous ideas. These ideas are dangerous. Instead, we believe in free speech, including online and including on campus."

With both his criticism—not censorship—of the press and reminder to publicly funded colleges of their stated missions, Trump is not seizing control of elements of the culture beyond his purview. He is barely altering policy. He is, however, sending a powerful cultural signal to two of the most important bastions of left-wing power that the rest of us are onto them.

For decades now, the institutionalized left has relied on the "tenured radicals" of academia not only to encourage campus activists—sometimes giving them time off or even class credit for left-wing activist activities but rarely for, say, Turning Point USA rallies—but also to train the nation's journalists.

You don't have to go to journalism school to pick up on the left's philosophy, either. It's in English classes. It's in history classes. Almost any college student in America in the twenty-first century knows what it's like to be told, in ways subtle and unsubtle, that there's a rough narrative that all good people agree upon about what America is and what one should expect each new story from the wider world to affirm.

You're free to say what you like, thank goodness, but unless you're naturally combative, you'll probably have been trained to be skeptical of tradition, religion, capitalism, individualism, the right to armed self-defense, conventional gender roles, or the classics of Western literature. In the place of all of those things—which not so long ago one might have summed up with the label "civilization"—there is the gospel of social justice, substituting, respectively, for each of those components of civilization: subversion, mysticism, socialism, collectivism, gun control, sixty-three genders, and postmodernism.

Who needs censorship, the cynical leftist might chuckle, when everyone in academia and media is on the same page anyway? To step out of line takes courage when it invites disapproval that can affect, in rough chronological order, your prospects for college admission, good grades, philosophical credibility, employment, and affirmation by the media establishment. Everyone from your teachers to social media executives is determined to behave as if the left-establishment's worldview is as unquestionable as mathematics or basic physics, and it's an effective strategy. People are prone to think as their peers do. If no one appears to be questioning a worldview, it remains dominant . . . at least for a while.

In pointing a finger at two of the pillars of the liberal establishment's dominance—academia and media—Trump is not threatening the First Amendment. He's showing us where the threats to those freedoms are likeliest to come from. Sooner or later, an establishment that hates to be questioned may like to make it official by writing it into law.

I don't expect the left to pass a law anytime soon saying that conservative books are banned—but keep in mind their ever-expanding definition of "hate" and their willingness to contemplate legal remedies to that state of mind.

While Trump gets lambasted unfairly as a threat to press freedom, the Federal Election Commission keeps openly contemplating the idea of cracking down on "misinformation"—as decided by them—that might affect the outcome of elections. I won't deny there's plenty of nonsense online, some of it from dubious sources, but if policing information for its political appropriateness isn't a formula for First Amendment violations, I don't know what is. We will regret going down that road if we insist on doing so.

I think if the debate were about censoring books or traditional print newspapers that contain political "misinformation," it would be more obvious, even to the left, how insane this line of thinking is. When it's slightly newer technology, the idea somehow seems more palatable, like a modernized regulation instead of a direct assault on a document ratified in 1787 and meant to endure for the ages.

Even now, DARPA, the Defense Advanced Research Projects Agency, is publicly discussing its plans to develop software to combat misleading memes. That means a think tank affiliated with the Defense Department, using taxpayers' dollars, will wage cyber war against what the government deems bad ideas, using algorithms to hide the fact that certain values are overriding certain other values, as if it were all just a matter of spotting certain letter combinations and numbers.

Meanwhile, TV journalist Chris Cuomo effectively threatens CNN viewers and his Twitter followers, telling them CNN has the right to view documents (such as those leaked to WikiLeaks) that the public does not and that "hate speech" is not protected by the First Amendment, which would be a big surprise to some sharp-tongued Founding Fathers and their political opponents.

And while the press itself—not Trump—erodes the idea of free speech, back on campus, activists partner with boring college administrators on hundreds of US college campuses to encourage the idea of anonymously reporting any remotely culturally biased statement to "bias response teams," which can lead to mandatory sensitivity training.

Ironically, over two centuries after fighting the British for the right to create our Constitution, it sounds like we're moving in the direction of creating speech cops who listen in on your conversation for insensitive or forbidden ideas, as police in England increasingly do. All for your protection, of course.

The Second Amendment

A well regulated militia being necessary to the security of a free state, the right of the people to keep and bear arms shall not be infringed.

A couple of generations ago, it was liberals and leftists who often claimed to be the guardians of the Constitution, especially of First Amendment speech protections, but they're rapidly losing interest in that amendment. The Second Amendment, by contrast, they never much liked to begin with.

Only recently have they become so bold as to suggest legislators should repeal the Second Amendment outright, something that is not very likely to happen in a nation with about one hundred million enthusiastic gun owners. But they are always chipping away at it, seizing every opportunity to press for new regulations, more restrictive background-check recommendations, more exaggerated mass-shooting stats, louder overreactions to gun-related tragedies, more sinister characterizations of average gun owners, more implausible post hoc rationalizations about which criminals would have been caught by which hypothetical screening methods, and endless "commonsense" proposals for seemingly minor regulations that in practice would make gun purchases nearly impossible and impose strange use, storage, and equipment standards for little or no safety reason.

It is striking how different the view of guns in rural America (where a disproportionate number of the conservatives are) is from the view of guns in urban centers (where a disproportionate number of the leftists are). Rural America knows most gun owners are harmless defenders of property, range shooters, or hunters, while urban America, still getting over its nightmares from the sky-high rates of gang violence thirty years ago, thinks guns spontaneously spark violent chaos if left unregulated for more than a few seconds. Urban dwellers have a very hard time imagining a gun in the hand of anyone other than a cop or a criminal—which means they feel very comfortable imagining the rest of us disarmed.

Given that President Trump is a New Yorker, then, we

should consider ourselves very lucky he didn't pick up the urban anti-gun impulse. He respects Americans' right to self-defense, and he respects the responsible nature of most legal gun owners over the federal government. He strays in tiny ways from the pure NRA stance of resistance to every new gun regulation proposal—but then, so does the NRA itself. Luckily, Trump's conservative supporters haven't been shy about holding his feet to the fire on the rare occasions when he sounds sympathetic to bump stock bans or social credit-checking for gun purchasers.

He has certainly signaled his sympathy for the nation's hunters and gun owners, in any case, and I had the honor of seeing that another member of the Trump family enjoys putting his gun rights into action: I've been alligator hunting with Donald Trump Jr. in the swamps of Louisiana, with that state's attorney general, Jeff Landry, plus Trump Jr.'s girlfriend, former Fox News host Kimberly Guilfoyle, and Sergio Gor from Senator Rand Paul's office. I first met the Trumps back in Chicago in person at one of Trump Sr.'s big rallies, little imagining I'd one day be with a member of the First Family in a setting so intimate and yet so far removed from their New York or D.C. homes, or other urban media and political environs. Neither Donald Jr. nor I were born woodsmen, needless to say, but he has become quite the avid hunter—probably a good influence on his father's thinking about guns.

I am learning. Paradoxical as it may sound to the non-hunter, you learn a greater respect for both the gun and the gator while you're out in the swamp. The protest banners we dimly recalled from back in the big cities and the piles of political literature wouldn't amount to much in this primal confrontation of lead and teeth. Even alligator hunting is a story of the little guy against the government. The alligator was put on the endangered species list in the 1970s and taken off in the 1980s. However, there were three-quarter of a million alligators when the government added it to the list. It was never genuinely endangered. The reason their population has grown to five million since is instead due to the careful work of local hunters, landowners, and farmers whose livelihoods depend on the successful protection of alligators.

You're happy to have a gun when you see a twelve-foot gator headed your way.

I used it, too. Don Jr. got an eleven-footer. Sergio got a ten, which he had mounted. And Kimberly made a pair of high heels out of the nine-footer she bagged.

Let no one tell you the only purpose for a gun is a government-run militia, police force, or military. Sometimes, whether against gator or human predator, you're on your own, as the frontier-expanding Founders well knew.

The Third Amendment

No Soldier shall, in time of peace be quartered in any house, without the consent of the Owner, nor in time of war, but in a manner to be prescribed by law.

Historian Gordon S. Wood has called the Third Amendment the least-litigated of all the amendments, and the Supreme Court has not based decisions on it. Not since at least the days of the Civil War has there been much call for soldiers to be quartered in Americans' homes, thank goodness.

Compared to many war-torn regions in the world, the United States has been an oasis of peace most of the time for over a century.

But the Third is one more reminder that Trump's aversion to unnecessary military conflicts has implications for the home front, not just for distant lands about which Americans may know little. In a sufficiently large-scale war, including one that began in a Latin American trouble spot such as Venezuela and spread across our porous southern border, there might well be sudden pressure to use Americans' homes as makeshift military installations.

None of us have seen the United States tempted to resort to such measures in our lifetimes, and I hope we never will, not even if it is done in an orderly fashion. This is not meant as any slight toward the military but as respect for the integrity of home and hearth.

The Fourth Amendment

The right of the people to be secure in their persons, houses, papers, and effects, against unreasonable searches and seizures, shall not be violated, and no Warrants shall issue, but upon probable cause, supported by Oath or affirmation, and particularly describing the place to be searched, and the persons or things to be seized.

The status of the Fourth Amendment is precarious in an era of increasing technological surveillance capacity by the government. In the early 1990s, the Supreme Court grappled for the first time with the question of whether watching a suspect's home with infrared FLIR goggles constitutes a search, for instance. If the only thing that counts as a search is the very old-fashioned method of stomping into a home and turning over tables, the government's perceived authority will be dangerously broad indeed.

And with each passing day, as whistle-blower Edward Snowden reminded the world in 2013, government's tools for watching and tracking us—not just as suspects but as innocent citizens going about our everyday business—grow ever more subtle and sophisticated.

As well-intentioned as the USA PATRIOT Act may have been in the wake of the September 11, 2001, terror attacks, its capacity to create a roving, ill-defined power of federal government surveillance over Americans has been recognized by critics on both the left and right. The USA Freedom Act of 2015 sought to narrow some of the powers granted to government in the PATRIOT Act in part by limiting the National Security Agency's power to collect bulk "metadata" on whole populations of non-suspects, the reasoning at the time of PATRIOT's passage having been that metadata is not in itself communications or user-generated messages.

But by now, most people have some idea just how much can be deduced about any of us, whether by government or industry, from the patterns of our communications alone—who we're connected to when, by what means, and for how long—even without the specific content of our messages being examined. The thought that the government might think it can continually collect such information from nearly everyone, instead of just precisely named specific criminal suspects for whom surveillance warrants have been written, is unsettling.

At the same time, the Freedom Act acknowledged the relatively reasonable case for continuing to allow roving wiretaps, in the sense that a known suspect might well pick up and discard numerous devices in the twenty-first century as a means of leaving a complex trail for law enforcement to follow.

So it is encouraging, though the issue has by no means been resolved, that as I write these words in the summer of 2019, Trump's outgoing director of national security, Dan Coats, acknowledged in a letter to Congress the suspension of the NSA's collection of call detail records but carefully specified the case for renewing the roving wire tape authority (as guided by FISA courts) and for treating "lone wolf" terrorist suspects as fitting targets for tracking even if they are guided by a foreign terror ideology without officially being members of a foreign terrorist organization.

We don't want the government to do whatever it likes in the name of national security, but we don't want to be killed by terrorists over a technicality either. Trump's basic sensibilities incline him to recognize this tension. He is skeptical of both government and red tape, not such contradictory impulses. He has also done admirably little grandstanding on these easily demagogued issues.

The Fifth Amendment

No person shall be held to answer for a capital, or otherwise infamous crime, unless on a presentment or

indictment of a Grand Jury, except in cases arising in
the land or naval forces, or in the Militia, when in actual service in time of War or public danger; nor shall
any person be subject for the same offence to be twice
put in jeopardy of life or limb; nor shall be compelled
in any criminal case to be a witness against himself,
nor be deprived of life, liberty, or property, without
due process of law; nor shall private property be taken
for public use, without just compensation.

Such a short time ago, the left's joke about the Trump
administration's relationship to this amendment probably
would have been the delusional prediction that the president
and his advisors will reaffirm the Fifth simply by having to
plead it when the Mueller investigation of purported Russian collusion leads to all of them being accused of crimes or
compelled to testify before Congress.

But both Donald Trump and Donald Trump Jr. seemed
to have the right attitude toward the Fifth even before the
Mueller investigation fizzled and devolved into the sad spec-
tacle of a distracted and exhausted-looking Robert Mueller
testifying to a Senate committee that he really had nothing
more to add to or say about his inconclusive report, the one
that so many Democrats had for months assumed would
show Trump being manipulated by the Russians. He must
have done something criminal, they "reasoned," since he's
just so . . . insufferable!

But long before things reached that point, Donald Trump Jr.
had said he wouldn't plead the Fifth if called upon to testify
even if it spared him an endless and pointless legal morass, since

pleading the Fifth might give the wrong impression. And he got that view of the matter from his dad, who had said repeatedly in the past that he thought it odd for innocent people to resort to pleading the Fifth. "The Mob takes the Fifth. If you're innocent, why are you taking the Fifth Amendment?" as Trump Sr. once put it.

Yet neither man seriously considered trying to alter the Fifth. And Donald Jr. handled his Senate testimony just fine without invoking it—testified twice, in fact, altering none of his original account of the whole crazy Russiagate tale. "It is all nonsense," as he summed up the Russia investigation after the Senate requested he testify a second time, maybe not having gotten quite the ratings or political bump they hoped for the first time.

The Constitution remains intact. It hasn't been invoked gratuitously. And the Trump administration can get back to work without the ludicrous drumbeat of an imagined coming Mueller revelation constantly in the background. Democrats will have to find something else to campaign on in 2020, if they know what's good for them. And Rachel Maddow's fading news show will need some new topics.

The Sixth Amendment

In all criminal prosecutions, the accused shall enjoy the right to a speedy and public trial, by an impartial jury of the State and district wherein the crime shall have been committed, which district shall have been previously ascertained by law, and to be informed of the nature and cause of the accusation; to be confronted

with the witnesses against him; to have compulsory
process for obtaining witnesses in his favor, and to have
the Assistance of Counsel for his defence.

You can't be a billionaire or a New York/New Jersey real
estate mogul, surrounded by regulations and competitors,
without ending up in a few lawsuits. Trump instinctively
understands, though, that everyone has a right to make his
case, to duke it out, and to deploy tough lawyers to do it, in
a fair court.

Gloria Allred, the famous feminist, left-wing lawyer, who
has harshly criticized Trump and once represented a transgender person who thought it unfair "she" was not allowed
to compete in an otherwise all-biologically-female beauty
pageant owned by Trump, nonetheless described a moment
that left her with a newfound appreciation for Trump's love
of a good, fair fight.

Trump bumped into Allred and another of her clients in
the green room at Fox News, Allred recounted in a Daily
Beast article. She recalls, "I introduced him to the client and
he said to her while I'm standing there with her: 'I just want
you to know, Ms., you have the best person you could ever
have. Gloria is absolutely relentless. She will fight to death
for you. She will never never give up. So never ever fire
her because you will never get anyone better.' I said, 'Well,
thank you very much,' and then he left and that's the last
time I ever saw Donald Trump."

Like boxing and presidential campaigns, legal battles
have their adversarial yet impartial rules, and Trump both
respects them and hopes to win.

The Seventh Amendment

In Suits at common law, where the value in controversy shall exceed twenty dollars, the right of trial by jury shall be preserved, and no fact tried by a jury, shall be otherwise re-examined in any Court of the United States, than according to the rules of the common law.

Liberals sometimes portray themselves as the guarantors of procedural justice—the ones who care about your right to remain silent, your right to vote. But over the past two centuries, the liberal tradition of defending those procedural rights has eroded. It has largely been replaced by liberals' faith in experts and officials. They aren't so much defending the little guy or the common person as the people in power who are supposed to know best.

I think you'll find many liberals and leftists look with envy at European court systems, where judges have great leeway, and the protections for the accused are more meager than they are here in the United States.

The populist wave, then, though it's so often depicted as an effort to cast aside normal rules—with the media endlessly misrepresenting Trump as a kind of spoiled toddler who wants to do everything his way no matter what law or White House etiquette say—is largely an effort to say citizen participation still matters.

It is no coincidence, I think, that it's largely populists (whether of a conservative or libertarian bent) who have kept alive the legal tradition of "jury nullification," which is the ultimate exercise of your right to trial by jury. Under jury nullification, controversial enough that some judges refuse to recognize it but praised by other judges in their standard instructions to jurors, even if a defendant has clearly committed the crime of which he is accused, the jury can in extraordinary circumstances vote "not guilty" anyway to punish the state instead of the accused—for creating an absurd law.

As our regulatory super-state grows out of control, and as we face the terrifying prospect of leftists someday creating laws as numerous and as punitive as their list of perceived "microaggressions," the right of juries to say "no" may become our vital last-ditch fallback tactic for resisting a socialist state. While Trump is in office, I worry about that a bit less. But the day may come.

Don't let them tell you it's the populists who want to railroad you.

The Eighth Amendment

Excessive bail shall not be required, nor excessive fines imposed, nor cruel and unusual punishments inflicted.

Trump Supreme Court appointees Neil Gorsuch and Brett Kavanaugh joined a unanimous court in overturning the Indiana State Supreme Court's affirmation of the seizure of a man's Land Rover as punishment for a small amount of illicit drug selling.

This Supreme Court decision sets a precedent for applying the Eighth's clause forbidding excessive fines (as incorporated into states' behavior by the Fourteenth Amendment) to *asset forfeiture cases*, and putting the brakes on asset forfeiture cases is a big win for property rights advocates. I am not dismissing the admirable goal of preventing drug abuse, but under asset forfeiture, a frequently used tactic in the war on drugs, police can preemptively seize your house or boat or car on the theory they *might* later learn those items were acquired with illicit drug profits or used in a drug-selling business. The incentive of police departments to play fast and loose with the rules about when and how you can reacquire your property is obvious, as is the perverse incentive of police departments to auction off the seized items for extra revenue—when they aren't just tooling around town in the seized cars themselves, as has been known to happen.

Seeing even the two new Trump-appointed conservative justices, whom the left paints as authoritarians, stick up for the accused against the grasping hands of the law is a reminder that Trump, though sympathetic to police, is not just appointing authoritarian "law-and-order" judges. Rather, he's appointing ones who respect both law *and* its proper limitations, the state and its bounds.

At the same time, these two Trump appointees have been an interesting living display of the comfort Trump-era conservatives feel with diversity of thought: CNBC notes that an empirical analysis by Adam Feldman, creator of the site Empirical SCOTUS, finds that no two justices appointed by the same president have disagreed with each other *more* than Gorsuch and Kavanaugh since JFK was president.

So much for conservative narrow-mindedness and homogeneity. There's more to the Supreme Court—and legal philosophy—than just right vs. left, thank goodness.

The Ninth Amendment

The enumeration in the Constitution, of certain rights, shall not be construed to deny or disparage others retained by the people.

Both left and right have been guilty of wanting the federal government to behave as if it can do anything it likes so long as that specific course of action hasn't been explicitly forbidden by the Constitution. Worse, plenty of people on both left and right are happy to override constitutional limitations on government power when they think some current issue is urgent enough—even though in all likelihood that issue will be forgotten a decade hence, and we will still need an intact Constitution to restrain government power.

To a leftist such as Heidi Schreck, writer of the recent play *What the Constitution Means to Me*, the Constitution is suspect because it was written by "white males," that charge being the acid in which everything about our society is being broken down lately. We can't change that past but can make the future more inclusive. Bring everyone aboard America's constitutional legal tradition; don't destroy that tradition. That's why the Constitution emphasizes individuals, not certain tribes or family lineages. It doesn't enshrine aristocrats as one official house of the legislature, for instance, while England's legal traditions did. People of all stripes have shaped the US Constitution's interpretation since its creation, and every individual benefits from the rights it enshrines. To leftist critics, though, its value is to be judged by its compatibility with present-day left-liberal cultural and policy goals.

That doesn't mean, though, that every conservative takes a strictly libertarian view of the constraints the Constitution imposes on the federal government, either. To a conservative such as Judge Robert Bork, whose own nomination to the Supreme Court was derailed by paranoid leftist criticisms in 1987 (a foretaste of the sort of opposition Trump appointee Brett Kavanaugh would face in 2018), progressive policy goals may not deserve special judicial deference, but the will of the popular majority does.

That idea has a certain populist appeal, especially if you consider out-of-control left-wing judges or other government officials. However, absent clear, strict limits on government power, it probably will be precisely those sorts of officials who end up imposing their will on the rest of us. Safer, then, to assume almost the opposite of what the leftists and the right-majoritarians do: Assume government can't do anything unless it's clearly spelled out in the Constitution. Not too many duties are: courts, defense, guaranteeing mail gets delivered, and not much else, which is for the best.

The Ninth Amendment, in short, affirms that if the Constitution didn't say otherwise, you as a free person probably have the federal right to do it. When in doubt, the federal government shouldn't act.

Reason.com senior editor Damon Root noted a slight difference in the way Trump's two Supreme Court appointees, Brett Kavanaugh and Neil Gorsuch, answered Ninth Amendment questions put to them in their Senate confirmation hearings, a difference that captures the tension within conservatism nicely but also reminds us both conservative approaches are probably safer than the left-wing impulse to read whatever you like into the Constitution.

Republican senator Ted Cruz asked Kavanaugh, "What do you make of the Ninth Amendment? . . . Robert Bork famously described it as an 'ink blot.' Do you share that assessment?"

Kavanaugh replied with a long, nuanced answer that contained this kernel: "So I think the Ninth Amendment, and the Privileges and Immunities Clause, and the Supreme Court's doctrine of substantive due process are three roads that someone might take that all really lead to the same destination under the precedent of the Supreme Court now, which is that the Supreme Court precedent protects certain unenumerated rights so long as the rights are, as the Supreme Court said in the *Glucksberg* case, rooted in history and tradition."

Not bad. Beats judges making it up at a whim. Gorsuch's answer on a related question was simpler, though. Democratic senator Chris Coons asked Gorsuch, "Do you believe the Constitution contains a right to privacy?"

Gorsuch replied, "Yes, Senator, I do."

Both men are on the right track, I think. In effect, one Trump appointee is saying that judges must defer to history and legal precedent. The other is saying the presumption leans against the government being able to tell individuals what they can do.

Both tradition and individual rights are safer guarantors of our constitutional liberties than the leftist temptation to exercise whatever government power is deemed necessary to prevent the social crisis of the moment, real or perceived. That way lies socialism.

The Tenth Amendment

The powers not delegated to the United States by the Constitution, nor prohibited by it to the States, are reserved to the States respectively, or to the people.

Much as the Ninth Amendment says, in effect, when in doubt defer to individual liberty, the Tenth says when in doubt defer to the states rather than the federal government, unless the Constitution or overwhelming constitutional legal precedent dictates otherwise.

Trump captured the spirit of the Tenth when asked in August 2019 by a *Washington Examiner* reporter whether cannabis might be legalized during his administration. Trump replied, "We're going to see what's going on. It's a very big subject, and right now we are allowing states to make that decision. A lot of states are making that decision, but we're allowing states to make that decision."

That's it. That's the proper humble attitude of a president running a federal government that does not pretend to be all-powerful. Trump wants to do what works, and he knows, as any admirer of the market should, that what works is best discovered through variety and experimentation, not a few experts getting together in Washington and telling everyone what to do. We are fortunate to have a conservative president who is more dedicated to that idea than he is to the more old-fashioned conservative impulse to smash druggies throughout the land.

Perhaps Trump's deference to the states is why he has so rarely been rebuked by the Supreme Court (and why I'm

encouraged by the fact that Trump has been able to virtually remake the judiciary with his numerous appointments
below the Supreme Court level). By contrast, vaunted President Obama, who came to the White House hailed as a
law professor specializing in the Constitution, was blocked
by the Supreme Court more often than he was affirmed. As
Ilya Shapiro noted in the Federalist, "Overall, the administration has managed a record of 79–96, a win rate of just
above 45 percent." His own appointed justices repeatedly
voted against him.

Maybe it's another case of the self-proclaimed experts
tending toward arrogance, chafing to see what they can get
away with. Trump wants to get the basic work of governing
done.

Obama, while talking like someone eager to restore civil
liberties purportedly eroded under President George W. Bush,
oversaw the administration with the most aggressive record
of persecuting and prosecuting leakers, whistle-blowers, and
journalists since the early days of the republic and the excesses
of the Alien and Sedition Acts.

With President Trump, we have traded a president and
inner circle who knew what they could get away with for an
administration that asks what needs to be done.

The MAGA Doctrine of limited government responsive
to the people (and not just its ruling elite) is even yielding
civil liberties benefits overseas. While the left tries to paint
Trump as xenophobic and bigoted against Muslims, the
Trump administration's ambassadors overseas gently work to
discourage anti-gay laws that can lead not to the mere denial
of marriage licenses (as in the United States until recently)
but to imprisonment and execution. Somehow that doesn't

stop the left reflexively claiming the Trump administration is oppressing gays (and everyone else). Reality doesn't matter, just sticking to the old tried-and-true leftist talking points from bygone eras.

Trump, as noted earlier, is the first president to enter office already supporting gay marriage. Obama did not, though he, like Secretary of State Hillary Clinton before him, supported gay marriage once it became apparent it was politically expedient to do so, given changing priorities among Democrat voters.

The MAGA Doctrine keeps America on a steady course toward greater freedom, greater prosperity, and more limited government, while its critics shift in the wind and congratulate themselves for their evolving views.

While conventional politicians rarely have any larger problems in mind to tackle than winning the next election, the Trump administration dares to think big. One of the best ways to secure the Bill of Rights, and the rest of the Constitution, for future generations is to appoint great judges. Let's look at how Trump has quietly been doing just that.

CHAPTER 14

Judicial Legacy

In addition to his two fantastic Supreme Court appointees, Neil Gorsuch and Brett Kavanaugh (the latter still plagued by the left's obsessive attacks on his alleged youthful behavior), Trump has been appointing good judges at all levels of the federal judiciary—over 150 as of late 2019.

This transformation of the courts may be Trump's true lasting legacy. We spend a great deal of time arguing about presidents and presidential candidates in the United States, but there are three branches of government, not just the executive but also the legislature and the judiciary. Trump's impact on the judiciary will continue even when his presidency is over and even if members of Congress who share his vision are all voted out of office. Most judges are lifetime appointments.

Trump's judicial appointments are one of the clearest pieces of evidence that he is not ideologically rudderless, too. His judges—including a shortlist of possible Supreme Court nominees he floated even before the 2016 election—tend not only to be conservatives but to be favorites of the Federalist Society, the widely respected libertarian/conservative organization that promotes open political debates about topics such as originalist interpretations of the Constitution—that is, the idea that the words of the texts should be interpreted by a familiarity with their meaning in the minds of the Founders, not just their sound to modern ears or their association with sometimes-dubious more recent left-wing analyses.

Though Trump has often had to butt heads with both the Democrat establishment and the establishment of his party, the swift confirmation of over 150 judges is solid work by the Republican majority in the Senate. As has been obvious since the Bork hearings of 1987, any judge's nomination can become the occasion for grandstanding and political spin by members of the Senate Judiciary Committee. A moderate can be made to sound like a radical if the politicians know there is enough media interest to echo the spin in confirmation hearings. There has been fairly little time for any of that with most of Trump's nominees.

Gorsuch and, obviously more so, Kavanaugh had to get through that gauntlet and will now likely shape American law for many years to come—but in a way, Trump's lower-court appointments are a more long-lasting gift. Their decisions may on average carry less weight than those of the Supreme Court, but many of them are in their thirties and forties, and they'll be deciding cases for decades (some, in all likelihood, from the Supreme Court as well one day).

The Senate even confirmed a few controversially conservative judges, such as Kentucky's John K. Bush, now of the Sixth Circuit Court of Appeals, who, in a reminder of changing times, was opposed by some senators more because of his decade of conservative blogging (pseudonymously) at the site Elephants in the Bluegrass. There, he opposed Obamacare (unlike Chief Justice Roberts) and likened abortion to slavery. He was confirmed, in part by explaining that his personal opinions on such matters would not affect his judging—and indeed, judicial philosophy is a different creature than political philosophy, hinging more on questions such as how much weight to give to precedent, when to send decisions back to lower courts, etc. Still, having conservatives on the bench is bound to affect the overall tenor of the judiciary.

The scrutiny gets stricter and the gauntlet tighter, sometimes absurdly so, at the Supreme Court level, of course. One thoroughly qualified candidate already feeling the pressure—considered by Trump for the slot on the Supreme Court that went to Kavanaugh and rumored to be on deck as a nominee if Justice Ruth Bader Ginsburg passes away, ghoulish as it may be to speculate—is Seventh Circuit Court of Appeals Judge Amy Coney Barrett.

Her 2017 confirmation hearings were a revealing look at how radical the litmus tests used by the Democrats are becoming. Barrett was essentially raked over the coals, in particular by longtime California senator Dianne Feinstein, for being Catholic, and for using the term "orthodox Catholic" to describe herself, as though over seventy million Americans, the single largest religious denomination in the United States, were some fringe group. The real imperative in the minds of Democrat interlocutors in such hearings is "Protect abortion at any cost," as if the whole of judicial philosophy and politics revolves around the odds that someone might push back against the post–*Roe v. Wade* legal regime. Like most judges, Barrett contends she will decide cases—on a wide array of issues—on their legal merits.

The current Supreme Court is already majority-Catholic, by the way, and it hasn't resulted in a rush to shoehorn the overturning of *Roe v. Wade* into every case. If you count Gorsuch (whose background includes both Catholicism and Episcopalianism) as Catholic, the Supreme Court is two-thirds Catholic, and they still appear to make their decisions based on solidly secular points of US legal tradition. Maybe Catholics are capable of rationally weighing legal philosophical arguments just like thinkers from any other sect. It's a little creepy to suggest they're all on a stealth mission, much as I love it when law reaffirms Americans' most basic right, the right to life. Senate confirmation hearings obviously can't be allowed to reinstitute ancient religious tests for participating in public life.

Trump's performance on judicial nominees is another great example of him exceeding expectations.

If he were as philosophically random and reckless as his critics, even some on the right, imply—if his only lodestar were "what helps Trump"—there would likely be no pattern to his appointments. The government is filled with people who are of no particular ideological interest but are "qualified" by dint of prior experience in similar positions. The coast to the political center is so easy when you make appointments out of non-threatening, familiar faces who seem to get along with everyone on both sides of the aisle. Presidents are constantly advised to save their ammunition for more important battles that never seem to arrive. Even in very contentious times, D.C.'s main unwritten rule is "Don't rock the boat."

Trump has just given the ship of state a much-needed tack to the right.

He has also done it without appointing hacks and cronies who might open him up to charges of caring about nothing but ideology. (His de facto advisors at the Federalist Society recognize the need for wisdom and experience in judges of any party.) NPR, seemingly grasping for some way to condemn the Trump appointments, was reduced to running a piece whining that the appointed judges are about 70% white males. However, only about a third of federal judges were female before Trump took office, and—though the country is getting more diverse all the time and diversity is indeed an asset—the United States is still about two-thirds white. White males will inevitably crop up from time to time, even if complaining about it has gotten a little more fashionable.

It doesn't tell us too much about how they'll decide cases, obviously—probably even less than their religious denominations would. Let's try to aim higher than simple demographics in debating judges' track records.

One of the strangest aspects of watching the left sit in judgment upon conservatives' legal objectivity, of course, is how lawless the left becomes once such hearings are over and politics as usual resumes.

Take the weird, belated attempt to rekindle accusations against Justice Kavanaugh late in the summer of 2019, well after he was safely seated on the Supreme Court. A book that had not yet been released quoted a lawyer who recollected hearing that friends of Kavanaugh, back in college, had shoved Kavanaugh's penis into a woman's hand. The woman admits she had no memory of such an incident, no other witnesses came forward—oh, and the man with the vague recollection of other people's recollections was Max Stier, a former lawyer for Bill Clinton who had defended him when Paula Jones sued him for sexual assault, Clinton ultimately paying her $850,000 to settle the case.

That doesn't sound like the most airtight case, from the most plausible source, against Justice Kavanaugh—but no matter. Numerous Democrats, including more than one 2020 presidential candidate, promptly called for Kavanaugh to be impeached! Democrats love impeachment now, but needless to say, they didn't back in Bill Clinton's day.

Instead of investigating Kavanaugh for an eighth time (the justice having been successfully vetted for several positions even before his Supreme Court appointment), maybe the FBI should investigate some of these unresolved scandals:

- Representative Ilhan Omar's immigration fraud (her only response to questions about whether she married her brother temporarily to speed up the process is to shout "racism")
- Representative Elijah Cummings's wife's shady non-profit (ironic for a member of the ethics-violations-policing House Oversight Committee)
- Senator Dianne Feinstein's assistant who was a Chinese spy (ironic for a member of the Senate Intelligence Committee)
- Representative Alexandria Ocasio-Cortez's campaign finance violations (ironic for someone who

thinks dirty capitalist money corrupts politics and society)

- Adam Schiff lying about Russia evidence (but maybe Russia is old hat and he has now moved on to lying about Ukraine evidence)

An added irony about Omar, by the way—one of the fiercest critics of Trump's wariness about Muslim terrorism and policy moves like his "travel ban"—she called for impeaching Trump well before it became a cause embraced by the House Democrats in general, ostensibly for campaign violations, though Trump hadn't been found guilty of any. Omar herself? Found guilty of at least six—and fined a mere $500 for it.

Don't let the Democrats get away with pretending to be the party of the impartial administration of justice, much as we'd all like to believe such impartiality prevails.

The left's politicization of the cause of justice is made all the more pernicious, of course, by hiding in mountains of seemingly objective procedure—and hiding it in the bureaucracy of the so-called Deep State, the mixture of permanent civil service, intelligence, and police agencies vast enough to generate its own cabals with their own political agendas.

Recall that even before Trump was elected, one of the text messages (dated September 2, 2016) from Lisa Page, an FBI attorney on Robert Mueller's investigative team, to the FBI's Peter Strzok reads: "POTUS wants to know everything we're doing." POTUS at that time, obviously, meant then–president of the United States Barack Obama. And she wrote that while she was preparing talking points for then-director of the FBI James Comey, later one of Trump's harshest—and as a glance through the selfies on his Twitter feed suggests, strangest—critics. Obama knew about the operation that had begun against Trump, on behalf of Hillary Clinton's cronies and other Trump enemies already ensconced within the ostensibly nonpartisan government bureaucracy.

In short, Obama presided over an intelligence community trampling normal rules and procedures to undermine Hillary's competition. These are the same people who went on to lecture us about propriety, ethics rules, corruption, and justice. Let's see Obama testify under oath about it all, and he might not seem quite so above-it-all as he pretends. Maybe Joe Biden would even have to stop touting Obama as a likely appointment to the Supreme Court. There are certainly some tough questions I'd like to see put to him in his confirmation hearings if he ever has any!

Maybe he could also be asked whether he thinks it's okay for Joe Biden's son to start a hedge fund with no experience, fly to China with his father, and rake in over a billion dollars in Chinese investments. Maybe he could be asked if there's anything fishy about Hunter Biden taking a $50,000 a month position on the board of a Ukrainian oil company with no relevant qualifications besides being the son of the sitting vice president. I'll bet he has some interesting thoughts on why it's illegal for American companies to hire the families of foreign officials but foreign companies can hire the children of American officials.

Until that hypothetical confirmation hearing, I will go on taking great pleasure in the ones President Trump has made possible. Every Trump confirmation feels like justice.

CHAPTER 15

Promises Kept

I suspect that what burns many members of the permanent (or formerly permanent?) political class about Trump is that unlike the rest of them, he might do what he says he's going to do. That wouldn't just result in policies the political establishment doesn't like—it would remind the public what frauds the other politicians are.

Trump has begun construction on literally his most concrete promise, the wall at the southern border. Trump is not opposed to all immigration. I am not opposed to all immigration. We are indeed "a nation of immigrants" in our historical roots.

It is also true that borders are, and must be, the first line of defense in conflict and a natural checkpoint when watching for criminal interlopers. Even the Democrats know this, though it is not in their electoral interest to say it too loudly these days.

Consider the strange legal limbo into which we have cast people in recent years victimized by cross-border criminals who our system refuses to oust from the country. If an illegal immigrant plays his cards right and neither gets deported nor treated as a domestic criminal, he might get off free in some cases.

Montgomery County, Maryland, is one "sanctuary" area for illegal aliens, and in September 2019, for the ninth time in just over a month, an illegal there was charged with a vicious sex crime with a minor—a twenty-one-year-old Honduran native charged with raping a six-year-old child. Democrat policies that insist we put electoral calculations and the rights of noncitizens before the interests of victims like that six-year-old are destroying America.

Trump is not hateful when he reacts to outrageous incidents like that one. He's angry. So are the rest of us—aside from the Democrats, who have no real interest in speaking for us. They certainly don't speak for all members of the ethnic minority populations whom they so often assert a unique right to represent. Consider:

- 56% of Hispanic Americans support denying permanent residency to migrants known to have used or are likely to use welfare
- 65% say illegal aliens shouldn't be allowed to draw from taxpayer-funded welfare
- 71% of black Americans agree

The indifference that liberal elites in this country and others would like people to show to their nation-states manifests itself in ways far subtler than the occasional horrific crime by an illegal immigrant, though. Consider the absurdity of the United States offering generous college scholarships, at taxpayer expense, to international students while so many hard-working American students have difficulty affording college, some deciding for purely financial reasons not to go (though I can think of plenty of cultural, noneconomic reasons to skip college).

Trump promised to govern as a nationalist, and he is keeping that promise whether the left likes it or not. Make no mistake, one should never equate someone who self-identifies as a nationalist with someone who identifies as a white nationalist. The media all too often are happy to make this false leap. Dozens of parties around the world call themselves the nationalist party yet have zero sympathy toward any racial preferences. There is nothing wrong with being proud of your nation, standing up for your nation, and believing in your nation first. That makes you a patriot. There is everything wrong with associating with white power groups or any other racially motivated group or party. In fact, these ridiculous racists explicitly choose race over nation in their rantings. Time and again I have denounced racial groups, white nationalists, and anyone who harbors hatred, yet the media seem to conveniently distort and ignore this fact. If you put being white ahead of being American, you have no place in the MAGA movement.

Putting America first is not the only big, brave promise Trump made—and has since been keeping, to many people's shock. Politicians so rarely keep their promises, after all, that it had almost become rude to hold them to their long-forgotten campaign comments. Most presidents decide they have to pick their battles. President Trump picks all the battles—and he doesn't stop fighting until he wins.

A few of the most important battles:

- The wall is being built. Despite skepticism from both the left and the occasional impatient conservative such as Ann Coulter, some 450 miles of border wall are expected to be finished by the end of 2020, along a roughly 2,000-mile US/Mexico border. Local officials in areas near the new wall construction report significant reductions in illegal crossings.

- The economy is booming. Every stock market has its ups and downs, but the market's early and emphatic endorsement of Trump's election has continued to pay off.

- ISIS has been defeated. The terrorist group's collapse was so abrupt after Trump took office one is tempted to conclude—at the risk of being smeared as un-American or a paranoiac who fears the intelligence sector—that Trump ordering the CIA to stop funding Syrian rebels made the crucial difference. By accident or design, money from the United States meant to find its way into the hands of anti-Assad rebels kept trickling over to that subset of the rebels allied with al-Qaeda or ISIS. Your terrorist enemies fare much worse when you stop paying and supplying them. If the old-school hawks learn nothing else from the Trump administration's foreign policy, let's hope they at least learn that one. And if they don't care, we have much bigger problems.

- Trade wars are quietly being won, despite media insistence to the contrary, as countries including China renegotiate tariffs and copyright-enforcement agreements to which Trump has drawn attention and about which he has talked tough. It may not go quickly, but there is no question China needs these deals more than we do.

- NAFTA has been scrapped and is being replaced, one of the most powerful symbols of the neoliberal /neoconservative post–Cold War globalist order undone by one man's nationalist vision.

- The Trans-Pacific Partnership has been withdrawn. By the time Trump scuttled that deal, you could almost hear the chorus of thousands of trade lawyers who'd worked out its elaborate quotas and sweetheart reciprocal deals crying out in agony. These deals have always been negotiated to benefit the powerful in each country, at the expense of the people in each country. Those days are over.

- Planned Parenthood funding has been decreased. The establishment of a true culture of life is a fight much deeper and more protracted than mere dollars and cents, but it is clear where the president stands on this core issue when presidents who talked more like conservatives did little to advance the pro-life cause. It is not a lost cause.

- The United States will withdraw from the Paris Climate Agreement at the end of 2020, assuming Trump is still in charge. We'll be free of all of those photo ops—and all that hot air—in Paris, and a world that treats climate fear almost as a new, unifying religion. Despite this, our nation's carbon footprint shrinks every year through innovation, not harassment.

- The Iran deal—under which Obama let Iran keep working on nukes while being paid vast amounts, receiving additional money in secret off-the-books shipments, and having sanctions lifted, all without stopping its terrorist activities and endless America-is-Satan rhetoric—was ended abruptly when Trump took office. Obama must have been pained to see yet another fragile piece of his dubious legacy fall apart, to America's benefit.

In fact, let's pause for a moment to remember the real legacy of Obama, this man who so many still talk about as if he were not just a good president but an inspiring, almost spiritual leader.

Obama gave billions to Iran and was willing to be quite sneaky about it.

Obama retrieved a US military traitor by exchanging him for terrorists who we released. So we gained a terrorist who now has to be cared for and monitored, and the terrorists gained several fighters destined to return to the battlefield.

Obama did nothing when ISIS took power in Iraq and Syria. As noted earlier, he arguably facilitated those horrible events by recklessly funding Syrian rebels.

Obama let Assad gas his citizens, even as we were supposedly drawing uncrossable red lines and demanding Syrian regime change. Embarrassing. Trump twice hit Assad's forces with missiles after he crossed that line.

Obama repeatedly embarrassed and shamed Israel, our

greatest ally. Trump, who some thought would be insufficiently supportive of Israel because of his noninterventionist tendencies, took the immense and unprecedented step of moving the US embassy in Israel to Jerusalem, a city of clashing Israeli and Palestinian claims. No wonder Trump is popular in Israel and considered an important ally by Netanyahu.

No foreign nation has found a greater friend in President Trump than Israel. That nation is a tiny miracle, surrounded by hostile, often theocratic Muslim nations. It is the one real democracy in a sea of totalitarianism and archaic monarchies. Israel has flourished spectacularly, its economic growth and contributions to the world unmatched by the other nations of the Middle East. It has virtually no oil, unlike its neighbors, and has been able to defeat countless attacks, repeated intifada attack campaigns, and even all-out wars.

It is a nation just a bit like Donald Trump: always surrounded by hostile neighbors, yet always moving ahead and winning.

As for Obama: He could have been worse. He was neither the far-left radical some of his conservative critics made him out to be—too friendly with big Wall Street donors for that, really—nor the capitalist neoliberal sellout that some of his disappointed left-wing critics charged. But he was handed an opportunity with his big win in 2008 to fix some longstanding problems in the United States, and for the most part, he just kicked the can down the road, sounding like a slightly less ambitious version of Bill Clinton.

When he failed to get the things he wanted, he constantly

blamed his predecessor, George W. Bush, or obstructionist Republicans in Congress. When he did get what he wanted, particularly his signature program, Obamacare, it imposed new burdens on already cash-strapped Americans—and had its key provision, the insurance-buying mandate, eliminated under his successor.

Obama is still talked about in warm, glowy terms by some voters, in particular many of my fellow millennials. But he didn't do that much for you (no thanks). Trump promised, and Trump delivered. His critics are angrier than if he'd reneged on every promise.

CHAPTER 16

The Great Agitator

One arena for fights between President Trump and his critics, an arena decidedly less dangerous than coups d'etat or
shooting wars, is Twitter. I know that there have been well-
meaning advisors to the president since he took office saying
that Twitter use might look unpresidential. It was entertaining during the 2016 campaign, but maybe he should stop
once he takes office.

I'm so happy that the president tweets, and not just because
that's the medium through which I expressed my enthusiasm
for him back in 2011 and 2012. I think it's natural for a president whose personality is such an important element of his
presidency—and who created the MAGA Doctrine largely
through his force of will—to communicate so directly with
his fellow citizens. What could be a better expression of his
brand of populism?

The people who claim Trump is autocratic should be

happiest of all about his Twitter use. You want to know what President Trump is thinking? I don't think you could ask for a more direct glimpse of his train of thought than that. It's direct, personal use of technology that was never available to presidents and citizens in the twentieth century, and it jibes perfectly with Trump's democratizing, decentralizing impulses.

Consider how abstract—and often how phony—political communications were in the last century. A few political philosophers and pundits gave you the idealized version of some faction's main argument in the form of a tidy manifesto, and its argument stood, in theory, for all time, contested only by other slowly crafted, infrequently published treatises. If people were lucky, perhaps they got a fuller look at what went on in their heads of states' heads years later when the heads of states' letters were published.

It may sound calmer and more stately than today's frenzy of communications and rapid-fire online arguments. But maybe that's why some terrible arguments and terrible philosophies lingered as long as they did. How long would Marxism have lasted if Karl Marx had been tweeting his basic ideas to the world way back in 1848 when he wrote *The Communist Manifesto*? A few tentative tweets might have entered his feed, and then a more market-oriented economics writer such as France's Frédéric Bastiat would have torn him apart.

Twitter can be ridiculous, but it can also be a crucible for getting at the truth—and shooting down nonsense—very quickly. We should be grateful we have a president so willing to show us his ongoing thought processes. True, Obama tweeted, but it's safe to say he didn't tweet in the Trump

fashion, sticking to safe topics, formally phrased. The difference between the two men online speaks volumes: Obama
cool and considered and still wrong, Trump spontaneous,
sometimes combative, but generally incensed about exactly
the right things (and people).

Trump's Twitter use is a little hint that he's achieved
something truly historic. He has reversed patterns of political change that seemed to be headed inexorably in one
direction for not just decades but thousands of years.

Think about it. From the days when villages first began
to be absorbed into empires, the world has grown more inti-
mately connected over larger and larger geographic distances.
Unfortunately, the growth of empires also meant that with
every expansion, there was a tendency toward the creation
of a more elite ruling class shaping the affairs of more distant
citizens. The twentieth century may have been the peak of
that process, with the British Empire, the trading and military
partners of the United States, the Soviet Union, and China
vying for spheres of influence. The independent nations of
Europe, whose clashes had produced many of our notions of
nationalism and democracy, were absorbed into the shaky
larger entity called the European Union. At the UN, particularly in its early, more naïve days, some delegates talked about
the idea of securing perpetual peace by creating a true world
government.

Only a killjoy, it seemed, would tell the global elite that this
process was headed anywhere other than toward tighter and
tighter unification. The idea that One World was our natural political destination was so woven into our culture that
it popped up in our thinking in many different areas, from
music ("We Are the World") to the children-holding-hands

designs favored by groups like the United Nations. To care deeply was to want a homogeneous, centrally planned world, all the smartest people seemed to be telling us for a long time, from the age of warrior-emperors to the age of the European Parliament.

But then cracks started to appear.

The United States was born in a separation from the most expansive empire the world ever knew, the British. The empires of Old Europe fell apart in World War I and World War II. The Soviet Union shattered due to an unworkable economic system, and its subsidiary republics quickly reasserted their independence, while Russia itself grew more nationalist and conventionally patriotic. Talk of world revolution faded. China struggled to keep a couple of its subordinate units, such as Tibet and Hong Kong, in line.

But the centrifugal force didn't stop there. As people on both left and right began to recognize that imperial dreams had suppressed local, traditional desires, it became newly intellectually acceptable once more to say that local determination might be a good thing, and those who aspired to rule everything from afar—from places like Geneva or Brussels— might not know everything. Greeks groaning under the restrictions imposed by membership in the Euro, Europe's shared new currency, began to hint at the unthinkable: that the process of European unification could be reversed. A member state was at least considering leaving.

Then, in June 2016, the United Kingdom shocked the world by voting to leave the European Union. Brexit could have been viewed as a mere local spat—the United Kingdom had always been stubbornly independent-minded. But interestingly, observers immediately took it as an indicator that Donald Trump could, just maybe, win the presidential election five months later.

In the old right/left terms, the two events would have seemed unconnected, but people were starting intuitively to recognize what was really at stake: mindless continued progress toward centralized bureaucracy or the reassertion of local autonomy. Dishonest commentators would point to the centrifugal force, and instead of calling it, as they well might have, anti-imperialist, they called it *racist*. Who wouldn't want to be ruled as part of a much larger, more international political unit, the liberal elite tastemakers asked? Surely, they concluded, only people so self-absorbed and hateful that they do not want to interact with the wider world.

But the word the left would have used in any earlier period for this trend of resistance to the center and the elite is still apt: *liberation*.

Donald Trump was the ultimate confirmation that what looked like an inevitable, "natural" political process—the watered-down twenty-first-century version of the nineteenth century's dialectic of Hegel or the twentieth century's acceptance of socialist revolutions throughout the developing world—could be stopped, even reversed. It is in *this* sense, not in the sense of turning the clock back to a time of greater intolerance or ignorance, that Donald Trump has stopped the Wheel of Time and shown it to be a gaudy and expendable prop.

No wonder the elite were scared. No wonder dozens of corporate jets flew to an emergency meeting in 2016 to discuss how to derail Trump's nomination to be the GOP's presidential candidate. Even many rank-and-file Republicans who (grudgingly at first in some cases) supported

Trump likely did not understand the real historic significance of his achievement in getting elected and his mission since. Trump wasn't just going to be a figurehead occupying the Oval Office. He wasn't just going to nudge American policy a few clicks to the right instead of the left.

Trump threatened to end the whole system of the world, by showing it didn't have to be accepted passively. The United States was not going to fade into a world government. The United Kingdom does not have to become the northern branch of Brussels. A different outcome to history was still possible, is still possible.

Trump, the America-loving nationalist, has global implications.

The analogies are readily apparent between this changed view of the globe, the changed view of military priorities that goes with it, and the attitude with which Trump-style populists view domestic US politics.

The recurring theme is a refusal to let vast, impersonal forces, masquerading as historical destiny, decide what will become of us.

The United States doesn't have to become China—or a mere extension of Latin America.

The world doesn't have to be subdued by a single military hegemon responsible for ending—or sometimes it seems more like starting—all conflicts.

And individual human initiative doesn't have to give way to rule by the central planners and the elite scolds.

On all these levels, we are still humans capable of reasserting ourselves and controlling our destinies. Is it any wonder that message resonated with so many people who had long felt alienated from the political process? Is it any wonder some very powerful, very smooth-talking experts would like us to go back to sleep? Think of all the things they would be on the verge of getting away with if we did, from population control to the elimination of vast portions of industry in the name of reducing greenhouse gases.

The big political picture, stretching back centuries, even millennia, is a little unsettling when you consider America's strange place in it. If the long-term elite goal, usually un-conscious but in more recent times quite conscious, was a unified, homogenized world, the United States continuing to assert its independence would be a colossal sticking point. But no nation truly asserts its right to independence without first feeling some measure of pride. If they could make us lose faith in America, they could absorb us into their larger designs for the world without a peep of objection.

The global elite needed America humbled. They loved Obama's so-called apology tour, his low-key bowing to world leaders, however well-intentioned and polite. It was one sign among many that America was finally learning to stop thinking of itself as special. It was a sign America was falling in line.

The United Nations and other international bodies are so often frustrated by America's skepticism about climate change or international wealth redistribution (two policies the elite have repeatedly tried to roll into one, developing nations being more likely to suffer climate-related damage if the worst predictions about global warming–related flooding were true). The last thing the UN needs is a United States full of go-it-alone survivalists or conservative gun collectors admiring their antique flintlocks, not to mention untamable businesspeople or flag-waving nationalists.

US nationalism has always been a threat to the larger scheme of globalist, internationalist rule-making. Now I'm not talking about hate groups such as white racists; the vision that Trump offers on nationalism has nothing to do with race. It's nationalism for the entire nation, for the United States of America, not for a particular group, race, religion, or sect. One nation, united versus globalist elites. No matter how often we point out this very important distinction, some on the left continue to falsely group these impulses together. It's not a conspiracy theory; it's the biggest, most obvious truth about global historical trends. That makes Donald Trump, in some people's eyes, the most dangerous man in history.

How do you keep a people's spirit of independence, of self-determination, alive? For starters, you give them a country worth defending. You *Make America Great Again*.

Other nations needn't fear—on the contrary, they should learn from our example, if we succeed. Much like the "shot heard 'round the world" that began the American Revolution but also inspired thoughts of resistance to imperial rule around the world, thoughts that would not come to fruition for most for another two centuries, the MAGA Doctrine is a jolt to the very organizing principles of the modern world. It is a refusal to accept our place. It is a refusal to accept mediocrity. It is a refusal to await instructions from on high—especially if "on high" means some consensus plan conceived in Brussels or at a special session of the UN.

You know, there's a hotel directly across from the United Nations headquarters in New York City called the Trump World Tower, and I think I'd feel much more at ease and have much more fun in the latter, in part because I wouldn't be there scheming to control the rest of the world's population. No one should be. Trump isn't. He wants everyone to chart their destiny, as he has.

Instead of imagining the world ruled with an iron fist by Trump, as the hysterical left has for the past four years, try instead imagining a world full of people each inspired to take charge of their own lives and to live as passionately, as fully, as productively, as Trump has. They say one of the reasons people liked Trump so much when he began appearing in presidential debates was that he seemed like a free man. In a world of the regulated and politically correct, he was still daring to speak his mind and do as he pleased. What if we all followed that example?

The MAGA Doctrine may be a nationalist, not a globalist, creed, but it has implications for the lives of people everywhere, just as Athenian democracy did, just as the American Revolution's historic overthrow of the monarchy did. In addition to giving us a glimpse of how to Make America Great Again, Trump has given us a glimpse of how to regain lost confidence and lost individualism and make ourselves great again—or at least keep trying. America should not impose its will upon the world, especially not by military force. But, by its example, it can help Make the World Great.

The nationalists of all nations, the individuals living under all regimes, and the strivers within all systems do share a common interest—without bowing to a common government or master. Each person in the world deserves the chance to develop himself to his fullest potential, potentially to live as large as President Donald J. Trump. On some level, they already know that will not happen if they live by defeatist philosophies that say we cannot compete, we cannot joke, we cannot build, we cannot feel pride, we cannot break from the pack and shine.

Whether a human being's goal is virtue, wealth, travel to the stars, a happy family, or amazing art, she must begin by accepting personal responsibility for the outcome. Survival can sometimes be eked out by following orders or letting the experts call the shots. Greatness, on the other hand, requires the liberty and the drive to make the most of yourself. I want to see my entire country free to try. I think we'll win.

CHAPTER 17

The Opposition to MAGA

Whether conservatives have embraced Trump or joined the recalcitrant "Never Trump" faction has hinged in large part on whether they saw our republic as desperate enough to need a heroic rescuer figure. Many donors, politicians, and pundits saw themselves as part of a stable establishment guiding the United States on its steady path to peace and prosperity.

Some establishment conservatives have by now been won over to siding with the people against the powerful. They're starting to realize they were drifting sleepily toward disaster, and Trump is daring to stage the rescue mission they had largely abandoned. Better to help him than to fight him.

It's a little painful and scary having to snap out of your stupor and fight the political battle at hand instead of just haughtily commenting on it. For the past few centuries, most of the modern political philosophies, very much including

Progressivism and conservatism, have shared the view that politics is a protracted struggle, a few metaphorical inches of territory gained or lost with each subsequent election or major policy decision. Even revolutionary doctrines such as Marxism gauged time in terms of centuries of political and industrial change.

As a culture, we convinced ourselves things would never really come to a head in our lifetimes. We didn't want to be arrogant by daring to think we were living at the crucial moment of decision. That's humble and healthy, but it made it easier to treat existing regulations, existing think tanks, familiar TV pundits, and all the rest as if they were permanent. No likelihood of change and thus no need to exert the effort necessary to make a change.

The slow decline began. And we were lucky enough to have one politician willing to rise up and say so.

The left-leaning parts of the establishment see Trump differently, to put it mildly.

The 2016 election was much more than a loss to them. Both parties have lost close elections before. This was something deeper, more primal, as if the slow drift of that ship of state, sometimes to the left and sometimes to the right—but gradually sinking—had abruptly been replaced by frenzied new activity on dry land. The left panicked, went through a period of denial, then processed their loss as trauma (there are so many stories of media and political professionals in Hillary's camp crying that night). They were entirely unable to see Trump as a jovial patriot and a defender of Joe Six-Pack against an increasingly tyrannical world. They could only see that as a façade hiding a secret fascist who would do the exact opposite of his campaign promises, starting wars, selling the country out to foreigners, and promoting the interests of the rich and powerful.

The most mature way to cope with the trauma would have been to ask how the Democratic Party could partner with Trump on those things about which they agreed with him and how it could oppose him in a respectful, civil fashion on the things that hopelessly divide the two parties.

The left decided instead to stick with "This can't be happening." Their intransigent opposition—pardon me, "Resistance"—to Trump since then can only be described as delusional. It will always still be 2015 in the hearts of some traumatized leftists. They cannot accept that Trump may have not just beaten Hillary but derailed their train, ended their dialectical process, steered progress in a very different direction, bent the "arc of history" at a new angle, and debunked so many things they believed to be inevitable—the empirical corollaries of the things they believed were desired by "all decent people."

Again, both parties have suffered losses before, but the usual reaction—the sane reaction, the healthy-for-democracy reaction—was to focus on making arguments that would persuade the public to support at least some of the minority party's legislative agenda. Can anyone deny that the Democrats after 2016, almost immediately, have instead poured most of their (highly) emotional energy into finding some way to prove that 2016 didn't happen?

The preferred culprit has shifted around—the imagined

demon who made this illusion of a Trump victory afflict us—but always it is as if *there has to be some explanation*. Sexism, racism, the unconstitutional Electoral College (which is laid out in the Constitution), xenophobic anti-Islam sentiment, and of course the Russians, the Russians, the Russians (and then Ukrainians, apparently). It is tempting at times for conservatives to think this left-wing fury and confusion is a great thing: Stay crazy and keep losing as America recoils in horror from the weeping, screaming protestors.

Trump has always sided with the underdog. He has always admired any David succeeding against a Goliath in any field. It is not a coincidence that Trump gets along well with visionary science-oriented entrepreneurs such as Peter Thiel (who was a Trump delegate at the 2016 Republican National Convention and later served on the executive committee of Trump's transition team) and Elon Musk (who discussed his Hyperloop idea for superfast train tunnels with Trump early in his first term). People like Thiel and Musk are in some ways the modern equivalent of classic American inventors whose creations in turn enabled other Americans: Edison, the Wright brothers, Samuel Morse, Jonas Salk, and so many more.

These sorts of people, and the divine creative spark they display, are the foundation of American greatness—not the perpetual lamentations and guilt-tripping of the left. Who really does more to alleviate poverty, to take just one of the genuine ills plaguing the world, someone like Cyrus McCormick, the inventor of the mechanical reaping machine, who helped radically lower the cost of food production, or the campus protestors saying poverty is a plot by the wealthy to oppress the rest of us, who cannot be expected to flourish in an unfair society? I think Trump senses, as many of us do, that we are at a tipping point in American cultural history at which our ability to create guilt-tripping campus protestors may far outstrip our ability to create Cyrus McCormicks.

That way lies ruin—and more poverty, no matter how loudly the protestors rail against it and display their concern. We won't colonize Mars by protesting, but we might get there surprisingly fast with an optimistic start-up mentality.

It may sound paradoxical, but I think conservatives are the people eager to embrace tomorrow, and the leftists are the ones who now want to dwell in sorrow on our past, thinking we can never transcend the worst parts of it.

Embrace tomorrow with the will to invent, to compete, and to Make America Great Again, and I'll bet we will be startled to discover how good life in this nation can be.

It is easy to forget how profoundly different the picture of the future carried around in the heads of many on the left is from the optimistic sketch above.

When someone on the left tells you that energy use must be curtailed, the birthrate must be lowered, national pride must be diminished, masculinity and bravery must be rejected, and Obama's apology tour of the world must be preferred to Trump's assertiveness, keep in mind the pessimism at the heart of their worldview. Many on the left think the world is dying due to industry-caused global warming.

Of course, they don't like to see anyone who seems proud or who seems to be having fun or who sounds as if he's expecting a rosy future! The left used "hope" as a slogan for a few years, but they treat hopefulness almost as if it's an obscenity. They think we should be dissecting and atoning for the American dream, not readying its next and greatest phase.

If you ask a believer in the MAGA Doctrine what the future looks like, assuming we win the war of ideas, that person will tell you about peace and prosperity. If you ask a typical leftist these days what the future looks like, they'll very nearly say that we don't have one. No wonder they're bitter.

I suspect optimism also contributes to the greater tolerance shown by Trump supporters. Many of us spent years thinking the country's political direction couldn't be altered but then had our eyes opened by Trump's election. Good things could still happen in this world! For all our worries, we're having fun now, and it's hard for others not to notice. Look at the Trump rallies. Remember the victory parties. Watch us laugh at some of those tweets.

Avoid engaging in Antifa-style violence, and we'll be happy to bring you along with us to the big Trump-themed party ahead. We don't want a world of constant fighting and enemies around every corner. We believe many of society's tensions will fade away naturally as increased prosperity and a renewed love of our culture infuses all sectors of society.

The left thinks if we carry on as we have, we're all going to be fighting to the death over scraps as we bake in the superheated atmosphere. That sounds like a very dark future. I don't think it's the one we're destined to experience. I think tomorrow's going to be great.

Before we can get to that bright future I was describing, we have to be aware that the president's detractors and the opponents of the MAGA Doctrine will fight us, and they've proven they're willing to fight dirty.

Unlike some people on the right lately, I do not counsel sinking to the left's level. That would be hard to do if they're willing to engage in online harassment, smear campaigns, and physical attacks in the street and on college campuses. Responding in kind would not set a good example for the future—and wouldn't be legal in some cases. If we want a future of peace and rational discourse, we need to practice those timeless virtues now.

Let them make their best, most honest argument for turning over control of our lives to the East Coast media, Twitter mobs, government red tape, international bureaucrats, and globalist billionaires. That's a debate we can win.

Many people will flock to our banner precisely because they see us behaving better than the far left. Our willingness to engage in rational conversation on campuses is already making a difference. Every time people try to shout us down, tear down our posters, or knock over our display tables, the undecided are reminded which side is trying to foster civilization and which side keeps veering into barbarism.

As I write this, much more subtle and unsettling tactics are being deployed against the president, though. Maybe by the time you read these words, you will know how that conflict played out and whether the president prevailed. I expect he will, as he almost always does in defiance of his detractors' predictions, but history has its moments of jarring backward motion, as I suggested earlier.

I worry about what will become of this country if Trump is ousted in the 2020 election or even before that by the Democrats' overhyped impeachment threats.

However, the MAGA Doctrine is larger than one man, however large he lives.

CHAPTER 18

Never Surrender

The doctrine underlying the Trump movement's effort to Make America Great Again is mostly implicit. There hasn't been a short checklist of political commandments in Trump's playbook, and he does operate on a sort of intuition at times. But as we look back over the major planks of Trump's thinking, we can see a set of recurring principles, ones that have also guided America as a whole during its history. Among others, those are:

- *Disruption of calcified systems is a good thing.* We haven't just faced one bad party but a static two-party cartel. President Trump is unafraid to go after both parties and both orthodoxies. If it doesn't make sense, he won't defend it for partisan sake.
- *Boldness, on issues ranging from trade to peacemaking, is preferable to timidity.* Patterns of behavior that

impoverish or kill may appear permanent only because no one has dared challenge them. President
Trump didn't run for office to slightly alter the
regulation books in Washington, he ran to change
the course of history and restore America's greatness. While others might have tinkered around
the edges, President Trump has never met a challenge too big to face.

- *Recognize that the wisdom of the ancients, such as
  Cicero, shapes the best aspects of our culture today.* We
  are not just the pawns of today's experts. We stand
  on the great wisdom of many that have come before us.

- *The foreign policy establishment can be as wrong as the
  domestic policy establishment.* A great nation does not
  waste trillions on never-ending wars. For decades,
  private citizen Donald Trump championed the idea
  we must put America first and shouldn't be wasting our precious resources on building around the
  world. The foreign policy establishment has been
  wrong for decades, and this president is unafraid to
  call them out on their failures.

- *Nationalism can be a philosophy of peace.* Loving one's
  own country does not mean attacking others. On
  the contrary, it means recognizing that each country will tend to pursue its own best interests, while
  we should often be suspicious of those who claim
  to speak selflessly for the whole world. President
  Trump ran to represent the rights of Americans on
  the global stage. He didn't run to rule the world.

Each leader is better if they do what is best for their nation. Globalist institutions such as the United Nations have done very little for our nation except drain our tax coffers.

- *A freed economy is a robust economy.* Get rid of taxes and regulations, and American ingenuity will soon raise standards of living more effectively than any government program. When government is out of the way, the economic engine of America roars.

- *America is not a mistake.* Patriotism is natural and good. The left tries to make us feel guilty about our past, our cultural inheritance, to soften us up and make us easier to control. We should be proud of being the best in the world. We should strive to be the best at all times.

- *America produces larger-than-life characters, and that is wonderful.* Trump is the kind of bold, experimenting giant that the Founders hoped would one day flourish in the United States. Let's not allow the left to turn us into cramped and cowardly shadows of our former selves.

- *A great nation wants justice for all people, not just a few.* Our laws have sometimes been too punitive, our prisons too crowded, and we can affirm conservative values and the rule of law even while showing mercy where we have failed to do so in the past.

- *Healthcare requires the sort of transparency and market freedom we see in other businesses.* Everything opaque tends to become a scam. America spent decades making healthcare an overlapping mess of government, markets, employers, and insurance companies. We can simplify and improve that important sector of the economy instead of layering on new mandates as Obamacare sought to do.

- *Civilization needs an array of fuel sources.* We cannot continue to be so afraid of oil and every other method of energy production that we end up "clean" but literally powerless.

- *Free speech is necessary for all problem-solving.* As Trump said, we can't fix society's problems if political correctness prevents us from even talking about them. And while we applaud the technical achievements of social media and computer companies, we should recognize their growing power to stifle and skew public discourse.

- *The Bill of Rights is still the law of the land.* The Constitution is our guide, and it enshrines principles that remain true no matter how far modern lawmakers might like to stray from them. The Constitution was not written for its times but written to stand the test of time.

- *A conservative judiciary is a practical link to our nation's core principles and the original intentions of its Founders.* The MAGA Doctrine is not, as some of the most vicious critics would say, a "strongman" philosophy of rule by whim. It is a restoration of the rule of law after too many decades of thinking we could safely leave most of the nation's decisions to unelected bureaucrats and elected legislators more enamored of the latest social justice fad than the traditions that have bequeathed us this great nation.

Many challenges lie ahead even if we hew closely to the MAGA Doctrine. There will be crises. There will be domestic turmoil. There will be foreign enemies even if we do not go looking for them. But I think President Trump has set a good and sometimes underappreciated example of how a brave person meets those challenges.

You greet challenges with actions, not just comforting words.

You tackle problems with practical strategies, not just hopes.

You give the public that has entrusted you with power victories, not just apologies and rationalizations.

Challenges bring growth, and growth is good. Challenges go hand in hand with building—and before all else, Trump is someone who builds.

Trump is also a man who never surrenders.

I know that to his detractors, that must sometimes look like stubbornness. They think he's the sort of person who can't admit errors and so has to be stopped by impeachment threats or electoral setbacks.

That's not quite right. He admits defeats—even does so with a self-deprecating laugh now and then. But he doesn't give up. He keeps striving for that win.

American resilience is a trait that has been admired and envied around the planet. We push ourselves harder than any other nation. We don't settle for second or third place. We never used to, anyway. And I don't think we're about to start doing so.

We are the inheritors of the tradition that set out across the frontier in the eighteenth and nineteenth centuries.

We are the nation that invented more devices than any other, from cars to global positioning systems—from televisions to radio telescopes.

We were first to the Moon.

Why do Saudi royals come to the United States for healthcare? It's because we continue to be pioneers in medicine.

We bankrupted the Soviet Union at the end of the Cold War, and we outmatched them at the Olympics numerous times before that.

Yet over the last two decades, we have seen a slow-emerging push, mostly from the left, to settle for second. Has your child come home with a participation ribbon or medal yet? If not, be thankful! We are nowadays told "everyone is a winner," even if no one competed and gave it their all.

If the left's mentality on "participation" and being a "winner" had been around in the days of George Washington, we might not have a nation today.

To understand who Donald J. Trump is, and what the Trump philosophy really is, you must believe in American exceptionalism, resilience, and perseverance.

The man is exceptional—entertaining America even while making his billions, being beloved even by most of those people he publicly fired.

The man is resilient. Sure, not every company he started flourished, but that's how business works. The distinction is, he never gave up.

Look at how not only Democrats but the former leaders of his party counseled him to give up, to drop out of the 2016 presidential race, to admit he wasn't even serious about it all.

Senator Bob Corker called Trump support "cultish." Mitt Romney warned that if Republicans nominated Trump, "the prospects for a safe and prosperous future are greatly diminished."

Then he got elected, and the investigations started from day one. In addition to the Mueller investigation, Trump faced investigations over petty matters from the House Judiciary Committee, the House Oversight Committee, Ways and Means, Intelligence, Financial Services, and more. From the beginning, the Democrats and some Republicans could not accept the legitimacy of this president. They made it a mission to destroy him and the progress that he has achieved, so long as doing so meant we would get a different person in the Oval Office. Can you imagine rooting against your nation because you dislike the president? Well, in today's world, some have openly called for the economy to tank and for things to go wrong because it might help prevent the reelection of this exceptional president. While liberals have harbored hate for him for a very long time, today they are quite open about it. This is shameful behavior.

You might disagree with our president, but to root for your nation to fail? To root for a recession? This is entirely new and unchartered territory. To those who don't believe in Trump Derangement Syndrome, I say it is very much real and in full force. TDS has overtaken entire sectors, from Hollywood to Congress. How many Hollywood elite stars think they are wonderful because during an award ceremony they got up and started swearing about our president? These coastal liberal elites lost, and they are in full denial and a state of rage over what they can do about it. Instead of presenting an alternative vision for America, the left has focused on hatred, impeachment, violence, and vulgar language. Pathetic behavior that will get them nowhere. (I wonder if they've even noticed that Hollywood has also thrived during his time in office. It's hard to see what they have to complain about.)

Democrats can't accept that he won. Democrats appear to be willing to spend all 1,460 days of his presidency talking about impeachment. President Trump doesn't give up, though, doesn't quit, and doesn't back down—and neither does America in the face of adversity.

Never give up, never surrender, and always go for the win.

CHAPTER 19

An American Heritage

As I look forward to a MAGA future, I also remember how I first started on the road toward conservatism.

I have a sixth-grade social studies teacher to thank—though not in the way one usually thanks teachers and other mentors. Deviating from the usual civics lessons around the time of the Iraq War's start, this teacher railed against then-president George W. Bush. I would come eventually to see the war in Iraq as a mistake myself and to see the Trump-era Republican Party as an improvement over the Republican Party of the Bushes.

But of course the teacher couldn't stop there. He went on to denounce the United States in general. He made the whole country's history sound like a litany of evil, from genocide to slavery to oppression of women, capped by imperialism and mistreatment of immigrants. That's a lot to foist on sixth-graders, though that's normal in schools these days.

You may have had similar experiences in childhood your-self. It was one of those moments in which you know the authority figure probably has most of his basic facts right, but you still have a nagging feeling that he's missing some-thing, something you can't immediately identify. You also know that even though you've only been alive and part of this country for a few years, you feel attacked. This place that you love and trust is being trashed.

It's not that you believe the United States can do no wrong. You don't dismiss the evils of slavery or think other terrible things from the history books are make-believe. You have a strong suspicion, though, that for all our mistakes, things worked out pretty well—not just for a few but for the population as a whole—eventually. There's something fundamentally good about the United States, at least as com-pared to so many troubled and brutal places throughout the world, throughout history.

Not just good about the United States—great.

The teacher wasn't suggesting everything about the United States was hopeless, either, but he made clear he thought that conservatives were leading the country down the wrong road. They were fools, he seemed to suggest, who thought in their arrogance that the country could do no wrong. The best hope for us all, then, was liberalism, and not just clas-sical liberalism but the left. A good dose of self-doubt and shame might rein in this country gone awry, and voting for the Democrats was probably step one, at least if we took se-riously the implied civics lesson underlying everything else we were hearing in social studies class.

I was a kid. I wasn't even sure what party my family was in. I guess I took it for granted the whole family would probably be in the same party, though I realize now that's not necessarily the case. I also realize now that expecting a sixth-grader to pick a party is probably unhealthy.

But I have a higher tolerance for politics than some people do. I kept thinking about the teacher's rant, was troubled by it, and resolved to talk to my parents about it when I got home. I suppose that means the teacher was doing his job in some sense. He got me thinking, though I could have done without so much guilt-tripping and moral pressure.

I asked Mom and Dad their party affiliation. Dad explained, contrary to what you might be expecting, that he and Mom were not steadfastly Republican Party–aligned. They voted Republican, yes, but they had other, much deeper loyalties, and if the Republicans went astray, they could well lose my parents' votes.

My parents said, among other things, that they were Christians and grateful Americans, and to the extent the Republicans captured those basic orientations, they felt a kinship to the Republican Party and would reward it with at least provisional loyalty. How could they be grateful to be Americans given all the terrible things I was learning about the United States in social studies class, though, and all the things the teacher was suggesting were true about a socially repressive, warmongering president like Bush?

My father explained how much larger the United States is than any given year's political controversies. The United States is the entire sweep of its centuries of history, including its proud tradition of protecting individual rights and its incredibly productive commercial culture.

Still, I needed something objective, something bigger than personal rootedness to a tradition. My interest in defending the legal and political institutions of the United States led, with encouragement from Dad, to me reading things like economist Milton Friedman's books, such as *Capitalism and Freedom* and (with his wife, Rose) *Free to Choose*. Friedman made the case that central planning is pitched to us as the answer to all our social ills, but for inescapable reasons rooted in the immutable laws of economics—which are really just logic applied to describing the way humans buy and sell things—central planning can never be as efficient as the individual, decentralized buying and selling decisions of billions of individuals.

You and I trade because one of us has something to sell and the other something to buy, and we both feel, in subjective ways no outsider can judge without knowing our internal mental processes and preferences, that we'll be better off from making the trade. Out of individual self-interest, we're cooperating to mutual advantage, which is supposed to be what leftists want the whole world to do. Unfortunately, they fail to see how profiting from trade can be compatible with that humane goal. They think if someone is making money, it must have been stolen from somewhere or that someone has been exploited. If everyone involved expresses happiness with the exchange, that's just proof they've been brainwashed by the system, in the know-it-all judgment of the left.

Friedman was clearly onto something, and throughout the second half of the twentieth century he made his arguments across different media with good humor and clarity, demonstrating that principles can be combined with effective communication, leading to political activism that made a real difference. Friedman was a big influence on the

United States moving toward somewhat more stable Federal Reserve interest rates, the end of the peacetime military draft, increased school choice, and skepticism even among conservatives about the efficacy of the drug war. Some of those positions were not—still are not—standard conservative views, but they obviously were rooted in the logic of markets, not some hatred of America. Friedman was making a conservative, free-market case for limited government.

He was also ahead of the curve in recognizing one of the big areas of contention in current conservative thinking: how to handle immigration. As a critic of regulation, someone who recognized that markets are global—and admired the free-market spirit of places like Hong Kong—Friedman preferred a virtually borderless world, but he argued that open borders are not compatible with an unrestrained welfare state that promises endless newcomers free goods extracted by force from the taxed populace. There had to be either an end to the welfare state or some limits on immigration. Perhaps one day when the entire apparatus of the modern welfare state has been turned into private and voluntary services, the United States can afford to let in everyone—everyone who abides by the rules of the marketplace and pays their own way—but until then, it's good to have a wall.

Reading Milton Friedman led me to read other thinkers who understood the interplay between economics and our political culture, among them Thomas Sowell, author of, among many other works, *The Vision of the Anointed*, about the way left-liberal intellectuals imagine themselves to be not just better informed but more moral than the rest of us— much as they hate to use the language of traditional morality. Sowell is a little closer than Friedman to the philosophical orientation of "Austrian School" economists such as Friedrich Hayek and Ludwig von Mises.

Sowell recognizes that it's not just innocent consumers and businesspeople who are tempted to turn to some socialist-style central planning mechanism, such as big government, to relieve them of the perceived risks of the marketplace. It's also the conniving central planners and all their dependents, whether in subsidized corporations, subsidized academic programs, or old media that thrive on intimate connections with high-placed sources in the political establishment. Add to them every intellectual who dreams, perversely, of being the one in charge and making a flawed society reshape itself according to the intellectual's whims.

A whole arrogant, well-off, smug stratum of society exists to replace your plans with its plans.

The numerous topics Sowell has addressed in his books include America's divisive racial politics, and admirably, instead of merely playing a race card of his own—Sowell is black—and insisting that his own personal experience is thus the be-all and end-all of evidence on the matter, he applies common sense and math in his book *Civil Rights: Rhetoric or Reality?* to show how even the most well-meaning businesses, including minority-owned businesses, will likely run afoul of affirmative action and antidiscrimination regulations at some point. Just as thrown dice will not always turn up the same number, the most random and color-blind hiring in the world will not always yield a workplace perfectly matched to the demographics of the wider society.

Then factor in all the real, historical—yet not hate-based—reasons for ethnic variations in choice of occupation that might produce different ethnic patterns in different businesses. Germans might be more interested in classical music than some other populations because of centuries-long family ties to traditions such as piano-making businesses. Chinese people, common sense suggests, might be slightly more interested in running Chinese restaurants than non-Chinese people—and there's nothing wrong with that! Not as long as we continue to get along with each other, exchanging goods and ideas. That's diverse America—not some artificially homogeneous, mathematically decreed experiment devised by the anointed moral arbiters of "social justice."

Through thinkers like Friedman and Sowell, I came to understand my own instinctual defense of America better. I wasn't trying to defend bad, dysfunctional aspects of the country. I was defending our capacity for constant, inspiring improvement, improvements made by free individuals, not socialist committees giving orders to the rest of us. Friedman and Sowell both understood that, and unlike some of my peers, they also came from a generation that remembers the horrible consequences in Europe and Asia last century from ignoring the lessons of free-market economics and individualism. They remember communism and fascism, and they haven't forgotten the toll.

Meanwhile, some Generation Z trolls would like to revive socialism with a hip new face like Alexandria Ocasio-Cortez on it, and some on the other side of the political divide would like to revive fascism but treat it like a big inside (and online) joke this time, as if that turns it into a good idea.

The best political idea is to stick to what made this country uniquely successful from the beginning, and it wasn't socialism or fascism. On the contrary, it was limited government, freedom to engage in commerce, avoidance of entangling military alliances, respect for the individual's rights, and an optimism born of boundless imaginative creativity. Those things made America great. We must not forget them. My parents remembered and changed my life by passing those ideas on to me, both by living according to those principles and pointing me toward the thinkers who make them more explicit.

By remembering those ideas, we aren't just winning the next election or defeating a few noisy pundits. We are honoring our ancestors, enriching the nation, and safeguarding our posterity. We are rising above the divisive current political squabbles to look at the big picture, which combines economics, constitutional law, culture, and individual integrity into the greatest formula for success humanity has yet devised.

We are Making America Great Again.

Acknowledgments

To the fantastic team at Turning Point USA: You are the best team in the entire movement. No one works harder and achieves more than you. We are changing the world for the better. We are shaping the future of this nation. Thank you for all that you do!

To President Trump: Thank you for saving our country and, unlike many who have come before you, keeping your word!

To Rush Limbaugh: Thank you for giving me a passion for conservatism from a young age. Your daily wisdom keeps me on the right track.

To Don Jr.: Thank you for everything you do for Turning Point USA and for your commitment to our country.

To Kimberly Guilfoyle: You've always been a star and will continue to be one. Thank you for making Turning Point USA shine!

To Jared and Ivanka: Thank you for your perseverance, which continues to deliver results, and for your incredible passion for making our world a better place. You sacrificed so much, and for that, the world will be a better place!

To my parents: Thank you for always believing in me, for always being there for me. I am grateful and love you both!

To Bill Montgomery: Thank you for the original encouragement and your belief in this unlikely vision and journey. I couldn't have done it without you!

To my close supporters Mike Miller, Mickey and Teresa Dunn, Tom Patrick, Tom Sodeika, Doug DeGroote, Jim Holden, Gentry Beach, Tommy Hicks, and Jeff Webb: You keep this movement alive. Each one of you is a patriot, and you strive to make the world a better place!

To my close friends who always have my back, Sergio Gor, Arthur Schwartz, and Andy Surabian: I will always appreciate all you do for me.

To my fantastic publishing team at Broadside Books, especially Eric Nelson and Theresa Dooley: Thank you for believing in me and enabling me to share my vision with the rest of the nation.

About the Author

Charlie Kirk is the founder and president of Turning Point USA, the largest and fastest growing conservative youth activist organization in the country with over 250,000 student members, over 150 full-time staff, and a presence on over 1,500 high school and college campuses nationwide. Charlie is also the chairman of Students for Trump, which aims to activate one million new college voters on campuses in battleground states in the lead-up to the 2020 presidential election. His social media reaches over 100 million people per month, and according to *Axios*, his is one of the top 10 most engaged Twitter handles in the world. He is also the host of *The Charlie Kirk Show*, which regularly ranks among the top news shows on Apple podcast charts.